TRIATHLON

NUTRITION

FOUNDATIONS

A System to Nail Your Triathlon Race Nutrition and Make It a Weapon on Race Day

"TRIATHLON TAREN" GESELL

Published worldwide by "Triathlon Taren" Gesell
Print ISBN: 978-1-7770901-3-5
Ebook ISBN: 978-1-7770901-4-2

Visit Amazon for other books by "TRIATHLON TAREN" GESELL

Triathlon Swimming Foundations

Triathlon Bike Foundations

Triathlon Running Foundations

CONTENTS

CHAPTER 1

INTRODUCTION

When I first started triathlon, I managed to avoid many of the nutritional disasters you commonly hear about in the endurance world. I never had to make an emergency porta-potty stop during a race, never sent a gel back out the way it came in, never miscalculated my caloric needs so badly that I had to walk half the run. But this was by sheer luck, and maybe thanks to an iron gut from my younger years of "stress testing" my digestive system with flats of beer and late-night, fast-food meals.

During my first few years in triathlon, I participated in Sprint and Olympic distance races. This masked my lack of knowledge about nutrition. I always made it across the finish line, albeit with some serious cramps, not much pep in my step, and a stomach ready to go on strike at any minute. I finished those races *despite* my lack of knowledge about race nutrition.

In my fifth season of endurance events, I decided to tackle a bigger challenge: an open water marathon swim of 27 non-stop kilometers (16.8 miles) from the town of Lac du Bonnet, Manitoba to Cape Coppermine where our family cottage was located. I had never done an endurance event longer than three hours before, and this swim would mark my transformation from an overweight party animal who was afraid of the water, to someone who takes care of myself physically and, as I like to say, drop-kicks my fears.

I gave myself nine months to prepare for the event. I would spend the first six months building up my strength with four 60 to 90-minute swims each week, and in the final three months, I would increase one of those swims by 10% each week. A couple of weeks before the marathon swim, I would I add a final 4.5-hour training swim, during which I'd have to take in a lot of calories, because swimming 27 kilometers burns a lot of energy.

As soon as I started stepping up the weekly long swim past 90 minutes, I started taking in more calories but I didn't really know what I was doing. This quickly became a problem. I started with gels and chews but since I didn't know how much to take, I bonked as I got close to the two-hour mark. I assumed I needed really dense calories, so I would sip Boost during my long swims, and that resulted in an upside-down gut that saw me farting in my wetsuit for the rest of the swim.

Week after week I bounced back and forth between bonking and nearly barfing in the water. I couldn't figure out the rate at which I needed to replenish my nutrition, or what I needed to take in. Meanwhile the marathon swim date was looming and I could barely make it past a two-hour swim without having gut issues so severe that I had to get out of the water.

About five weeks out from the marathon swim, I discovered research which listed the caloric burn for a number of the world's most popular sports. The research was based on how much you weigh and how fast you're moving. Then I came upon some other research which said athletes can realistically replace around 25% of the calories they burn during exercise. Was it as simple as calculating the calories I would burn during the swim and consuming 25% of that number?

I did some rough math and calculated the calories I would burn each hour during the swim. I figured out how much I needed to take in from food (that didn't upset my stomach) to reach 25% of the number of calories I'd be burning.

The moment I dialed into my caloric needs, my long swims became incredibly easy. I could swim for hours on end. My gut didn't feel overloaded. I could swim as easily as I could walk. The entire process of training became so effortless that the hardest thing to endure was my cheeks getting sore from blowing bubbles for an extended period.

I ended up finishing that open water marathon swim in nearly eight hours, and I honestly felt I could have swam for another eight. This wasn't because I was such a great swimmer, rather it was because I knew my body's energy requirements and as long as I kept putting in the right fuel, my motor would keep running.

I realized since the calculations worked so well for swimming, perhaps they would also work for long bike and run workouts. Maybe they would even work for a triathlon. I spent a couple of weeks inputting the calories burned during various exercises and researching average finish times for the swim, bike, and run disciplines of every triathlon distance.

The result was a calculator that required just three inputs: my weight, the type of exercise, and the time I'd be exercising or my expected finish time. Voila! Out would pop the exact calories I would burn and how many calories I needed to replace.

I tested this method in race after race, workout after workout. It didn't matter if I was doing an intense Sprint or Olympic distance triathlon or going for a four-hour bike ride--I never once had stomach distress or bonked. Literally, not even once.

Cramps became a thing of the past, and muscle failure during hard efforts was almost non-existent. And this didn't just work for me: to date, more than five thousand athletes have used this calculator to dial in their race and workout nutrition. We get hundreds of messages from athletes telling us they can work out longer, and their races are getting more enjoyable because nutrition is no longer holding them back.

This book isn't just about that calculator, though. If that was the case, I'd just give you the calculator and let you use it the same way those 5,000+ athletes have already done. The calculator just provides you with your unique starting point so you can ensure you're in the ballpark of a proper nutrition strategy. You still need to know how to deal with workout nutrition vs race nutrition, what to do during hot vs cold weather races, what happens if you have an upset stomach during a race despite following the plan, and what happens if during a race you still cramp? There's also the huge question of whether you should go low-carb in training and if so, what do you take on during a race?

What you're going to receive from this book are not just the basics of how many calories and how much fluid to take in during a race. You're going to receive a total system for how to dial in your individual race nutrition strategy for absolutely any race distance from Sprint to IRONMAN, and how to execute that nutrition system on race day when things often go awry.

As Mike Tyson once said, "Everyone has a plan until they get punched in the face." I'm going to give you that plan, tell you how to dodge oncoming punches as best as possible, and how to counter-punch if you catch one on the chin.

Once you've gone through this book and have implemented the system into your own training and racing, nutrition will no longer hold you back from getting across the finish line with a fist bump, feeling strong and knowing you did your best.

Belly up to the table and let's dig in!

CHAPTER 2

THE IMPORTANCE OF GETTING IT RIGHT

Before we take a deep dive into this race and workout nutrition system, I want to touch on just how important it is to get your race nutrition right. This is a story from a TeamTrainiac.com member whose race experience might sound familiar to some of you:

"...Aside from the training and equipment, I also made numerous errors involving nutrition, assuming I could just pack a bunch of food and eat when I felt hungry. I didn't consider timing or what I'd be consuming, I just filled my bags with protein bars and hoped for the best. In fact, I screwed this part up before even making it to the starting line. Right after waking up, I decided to start my day with a pre-workout supplement, the kind bodybuilders use, full of caffeine and

liquid rage... which I immediately regretted as the swim start was delayed by an hour due to fog. As I stood there on the beach, listening to my heartbeat and running back to pee every 10 minutes, I started to realize I might be in trouble.

"I did finish the race, but it was fourteen hours, fifty-seven minutes and thirty-five seconds of learning things the hard way. Some logistically, like sighting appropriately for the swim. Others of my own stupidity, like how many cans of Red Bull is too many cans of Red Bull, regardless of how cute the girl handing them out might be.

"The point I'm trying to establish isn't to make light of my own experience, but to shed light on how a newcomer to this sport could easily emulate similar mistakes and quickly become discouraged or frustrated."

This approach is very common. Triathletes will often train excessively for the swim, bike, and run. They'll obsess over their bike gear, and research everything they possibly can about which wetsuit or pair of running shoes to buy. They might even train their brain through visualization. But when it comes to nutrition, athletes often overlook how important it is, and just buy a bunch of gels at the race expo to shove into their kit the night before the race.

Even seasoned triathletes are guilty of this. I met one of my best friends and training partners, "Super Dave" Lipchen, Head Coach of the Windburn Multi-Sport Academy and a 2:01 Olympic distance athlete, when he passed me running out of T2 in a race, only to immediately turn the corner and throw up a red gel (I still remember the color).

Sarah True, two-time Olympian and one of the best long course triathletes in the world, said on our podcast that when she stepped up to long course racing, she would often forget about nutrition. She would end up feeling completely famished at the beginning of the run and fade quickly, because she forgot to eat.

So many athletes -- elite and amateur, experienced or brand new to the sport -- consistently look at nutrition as an afterthought. They train like crazy and obsess over everything except nutrition. Two things are odd about this.

First, without proper fuel, how can an athlete expect to perform adequately, let alone well? Our energy comes from food and fluid. So how can we possibly exert peak amounts of energy for long periods of time without the right food and fluid?

Second, the stomach needs to be trained just like the rest of the body, perhaps even more. When we perform physical activity, our digestive system doesn't function very well because the blood in our body is being used to power our limbs, so there's little blood available for our digestive functions. In order to digest our food and fluid during a race, our digestive system needs to be properly trained to make sure it can function optimally while in this impaired state.

All this said, nutrition is a common thing to overlook, so don't feel bad if you haven't put much focus on it. But it is a critical aspect of your overall triathlon training/racing plan and you need to get right. Ignoring it will be to your detriment. We hope through the system outlined here, that you won't ever get hungry and fade during a race, or have to puke up a red gel at the edge of a transition area (though if you do, maybe you'll make a new friend in the process).

CHAPTER 3

CLARIFY YOUR NUTRITION

Triathlon race nutrition is often seen as a mythical beast that athletes need to tame. Then, just when they think they've got the twelve-headed dragon of race nutrition nailed down, the beast rears its ugly head again and the athlete goes through severe GI issues, cramping, or fading at the end of a race.

Race nutrition is actually a very simple problem to solve, but sometimes the nuances lead athletes astray. Take for example this old rule of thumb: if a triathlete is fuelling with gels, they should simply take one gel every 30 minutes. And here's where the issues arise. Is the 30-minute time interval based on 110 calorie or 80 calorie gels? Is the gel made from maltodextrin or fructose? Should you take fewer gels or any gels at all if you're also consuming a calorie-rich drink?

Let's make triathlon nutrition as simple as possible for you. If you understand just one overall concept and forget all the hype surrounding triathlon race nutrition, you'll be well ahead of most of your competition. Here is what you need to accomplish with your race and training nutrition to perform well:

YOUR RACE NUTRITION NEEDS TO REPLACE:

- ROUGHLY 25% OF THE CALORIES YOU'LL BURN;

- ENOUGH FLUIDS TO KEEP YOU FROM LOSING MORE THAN 3% OF YOUR BODY WEIGHT; AND

- ENOUGH ELECTROLYTES TO KEEP YOUR BLOOD PRESSURE STABLE.

That's it. Race nutrition is not about supercharging yourself on race day, or dilating your blood vessels, or being a fat burning machine, or whatever certain sports nutrition companies are claiming their supplements will do for you. Yes, there are absolutely some sport supplements worth taking to enhance triathlon performance, but that's part of the final 1% of things to worry about. We want to focus on the broader nutrition *principles* which are easy to implement and cover 99% of the requirements for optimal endurance sports performance.

The options athletes can use to fuel for races are endless, and this understandably creates confusion. The confusion leads to athletes not having a set plan for their race nutrition, which in turn means they probably didn't have a set plan for their training nutrition, which inevitably means their stomach is not remotely trained to deal with race day.

We're about to get into some basic principles of triathlon nutrition. These guidelines will likely get you 90% of the way to an ideal race nutrition strategy. They've worked for thousands of people across multiple different distances. However, these guidelines are not a substitute for personal experimentation which is what will get you 100% of the way to your ideal race nutrition strategy. Combine these guidelines with some personal trial and error and you'll be able to race anywhere, any distance, with any type of gel, drink, bar, or chew, from almost any manufacturer. Race nutrition should never be a factor that holds you back.

Here are the broad guidelines (we'll get into the specifics of each below because it's very important to understand the "whys" behind these recommendations):

1. Aim to replace 25% of your caloric expenditure during the race.

2. Sip a light electrolyte drink every 5 minutes totalling approximately one large bottle every hour.

3. Consume your calories in even intervals, every 18 to 35 minutes depending on your preferred race nutrition products and your unique caloric requirements.

4. Ensure your race nutrition comes from easily digestible sources.

To make this easy on you, we've created a custom race nutrition calculator you can access for free at triathlontaren.com/nutritionfoundations. You'll be able to calculate a customized caloric intake and race nutrition schedule automatically. Make sure to go grab that calculator if you haven't already because getting these calculations exactly right is critical.

I'll now dive into each of the keys to triathlon nutrition in more detail.

1) REPLACE 25% OF THE CALORIES YOU'LL BURN DURING YOUR RACE

Step one in your triathlon race nutrition planning is figuring out how many calories you'll burn over the course of your race. This is your baseline, the absolute starting point that is unique to you. Forget about the serving sizes listed on packages of sports nutrition products, you're the one that's burning the calories so regardless of what the packaging says, start with finding out how many calories YOU will burn in a race.

This caloric burn needs to be calculated to both your bodyweight and your pace—if you leave either of those two factors out of the equation, you could be 10, 20, or even 30 percent away from the correct number, which could lead to big problems.

In the chapter on calculating your race nutrition, we'll provide you with a caloric burn table as well as a spreadsheet calculator you can use to get this exact figure.

Once you've calculated your unique caloric expenditure, you'll have the basis for your custom race nutrition plan. Next, you'll want to take that number and multiply it by .25 to reach the number of calories you'll need to consume during your race.

For example, a male or female triathlete weighing 180 pounds completing a Sprint triathlon in 1 hour and 45 minutes will burn approximately 1205 calories, so they should try to replace 301 calories (1205 x .25 = 301 calories) during the race for the best performance.

The 25% figure is derived from studies which show 25% is the approximate sweet spot athletes are able to consume during exercise without feeling bloated (the bloat happens when athletes take on too many calories that the stomach can't digest, and not enough calories to fuel the exercise).

2) SIP A LIGHT ELECTROLYTE DRINK

"Calculate your sweat rate."

"Weigh yourself before and after a workout and make sure you drink enough so you don't lose more than 3% of your bodyweight during exercise."

"Are you a salty sweater or a heavy sweater?"

These are things triathletes often hear when they start examining how much fluid they should take on during a race.

But it's important to emphasize those things are part of a very scientific approach to hydration. While this scientific approach is perfectly valid for professional triathletes with an endless budget and a team dedicated to their health concerns year-round, it's far too complicated for most amateur triathletes to use come race day. What if you're sweating more on race day and your previously calculated fluid requirement is way off? Are you able to hop on a scale and find out how much weight you're losing DURING a race so you can hydrate accordingly? Of course not.

Albert Einstein said everything should be made as simple as possible, but no simpler. We're here to provide you with a simple yet effective approach ANYONE can employ.

Find a large water bottle, something that can fit 26 fl. oz. or 769 ml. Fill it with water and a light electrolyte drink which contains no more than 50 calories per bottle. Products like Skratch, SOS Rehydrate, or Osmo Nutrition are great because they provide a great amount of electrolytes with just enough calories to help absorb both the electrolytes and the fluid (a small amount of calories helps the body absorb fluid and electrolytes, while too many calories impairs fluid and electrolyte absorption).

Take a big sip of the water bottle every five minutes when you're racing or training. That sip, and the rate of sipping, should be large enough that you finish one bottle per hour. This is your baseline.

Here is where you start customizing your personal fluid intake requirements. If you find you're burping or feeling fluid slosh around in your stomach, space out the sips more or take smaller sips. If you find you're thirsty, drink a little more. Repeat this process over many training sessions and you'll develop the habit of drinking at a good rate of intake without having to think about it.

When you get to a race, use the same approach. Dial your rate of fluid intake up or down based on what your stomach tells you.

Easy, right? Einstein would be proud. We'll get into some nuances of fluids and electrolytes later so you'll be able further customize your fluid intake.

3) TAKE YOUR CALORIES AT EVEN INTERVALS

When you're training or racing at a high level, your stomach's ability to digest food is impaired. When we exercise at a high level, our bodies take blood away from non-critical functions (digesting food), instead sending blood to power other critical functions (turning over our legs and arms). Because our stomach is in such an impaired state, we can only give it small amounts of food to digest.

For this reason, we want to space out our calories enough to not overload our stomach, nor to interfere with absorbing fluids.

Most sports nutrition products are packaged in doses such that when you calculate the number of calories you require during a race, you'll end up with an eating interval somewhere between 18 and 35 minutes. The shorter end of this feeding interval is ideal, while the higher end of that range is probably a bit too long and requires taking on smaller servings at more frequent intervals.

The ideal time interval at which to take your race nutrition calories is around 20 minutes. This is frequent enough to keep your mind engaged in the race while featuring small enough doses that it's very easy for your stomach to digest, but not so frequent that it interferes with absorbing fluid.

We'll talk even more about nailing down your ideal feeding interval later on.

4) GET YOUR NUTRITION FROM EASILY DIGESTIBLE SOURCES

While this seems like a simple point, it's actually the most individual element we talk about in this book because what's easily digestible for one person might make another person throw up. There are, however, some broad principles triathletes can follow that will help them find easily digestible calorie sources.

The two biggest principles triathletes need to understand when it comes to finding easily digestible calorie sources are:

1. Food should not cause gastrointestinal (GI) distress which is either felt by the athlete or are imperceptible to the athlete but still challenging for the stomach;

2. Food should not feel like it sits in your stomach.

These two principles will guide us into choosing sports nutrition products, or even natural sources of calories, fluids, and electrolytes, that promote optimal performance without adding additional stress to the body.

"BOCTAOE"

Scott Adams, the creator of the Dilbert comics, used to end a lot of his pieces with the acronym "BOCTAOE" which means *But Of Course There Are Obvious Exceptions*. That is very relevant to this book.

Scott Adams, creator of the Dilbert *comics. Photo used with permission.*

Maybe you're a triathlete who can't stomach anything besides water. Perhaps you're a full-on fruitarian and will only eat fruit for your calorie intake. Maybe you tend to cramp a lot and have had success with pickle juice to avoid cramps.

When it comes to triathlon nutrition, there's an unlimited number of potential options and challenges you could be faced with. What we're addressing is a nutritional strategy which will work for 90% of the athletes training and competing. Hopefully these broad principles will allow people with unique circumstances, needs, or restrictions to customize their own approach to triathlon race nutrition.

Remember all we need to do with triathlon nutrition is take in 25% of the calories we burn, enough fluid to prevent a weight loss of more than 3%, and to take in the correct amount of electrolytes to keep our blood pressure in check. Whether you accomplish this with processed foods, natural sources or a combination of both is up to you (and you alone.)

As you start going through the process of calculating your race nutrition, you're going to meet many challenges. The world does not make this task easy for you.

Sports nutrition companies are always touting the incredible benefits of using their "new and improved" formulations. Some of these claims are valid and some are not. Some are beneficial in certain circumstances and some are never beneficial. Take beet juice as an example. Beet juice has been proven to improve performance in endurance sports...but only for a subset of the population amounting to around 25 to 30% of triathletes. So, should people try beet juice to see if it helps? Sure. Just remember many of these supplement claims will only produce a marginal improvement and should never be a replacement for getting the basics right.

Bloggers and social media influencers are always talking about how the key to their success is "insert latest fad here." I'm guilty of adding to this noise with the low carb training approach I used in my build-up to Challenge Roth in 2019. However, I always tried to make it clear that the low carb approach was something I was testing for myself as a learning exercise, and it was not necessarily the answer to everyone's endurance racing problems. I also made it very clear the approach would not work for everyone.

I could have acquired more followers if I had called myself "Keto Triathlon Taren" when I tried the lower carb diet, or "Vegan Triathlon Taren" when I reduced meat consumption to see if my recovery would improve. However, fanatic claims that there is only one right way to fuel and eat, ignore the fact every person is unique. Instead of a pigeon-holed diet, people need broad principles that can be customized to apply to any style of eating.

In this section, I'm going to clarify some of the biggest misconceptions about triathlon race nutrition. This is important to do before we get into key nutrition principles because we need to have a similar framework of understanding about commonly shared "advice." Without clarifying some of these misconceptions, the entire rest of the book might not land well with you.

I'll try my best to keep this section updated in future versions of this book as new nutrition fads and topics come out. Here goes, let's poke the proverbial "sports nutrition bear...."

I'LL FIGURE IT OUT ON RACE DAY

As I mentioned before, the stomach and digestive system is quite taxed when we exercise intensely or race. The digestive system has less access to blood during exercise, and all the jostling around taxes the digestive system. The stomach is a muscular organ, so just like with other muscle tissues, we need to train it to perform on race day.

A friend of mine decided to get into triathlon and he did all the training necessary to complete his first half-IRONMAN, except the nutrition. A couple weeks before the race, another friend told him, "Oh, nutrition is easy. You just follow the instructions on this bag of all-in-one fluid, electrolyte, and calorie replacement drink."

My friend went into the race and everything that could go wrong nutritionally went wrong. He faded badly during the end of the bike leg, he had cramps during the run, he stopped sweating during the run but was really thirsty indicating he was dehydrated, and in the end, he finished probably 30 minutes slower than what I would call his "safety time."

We'll talk about problems that come along with all-in-one nutrition products later, but for now I'll say one thing about my friend's approach: even if he had the right nutrition requirements from that all-in-one product, he wouldn't have been able to absorb it because he had never trained his stomach to do so.

Most workouts longer than 90 minutes require a nutrition plan. Practicing your nutrition plan during your longer workouts is a perfect chance for you to start figuring out what does and what doesn't work for your body. It's also a chance for your body to learn how to digest fluids and food while exercising.

CARB LOADING

Ever see the episode of *The Office* where Michael Scott downs a plate of Fettuccine Alfredo just before running a 5K charity race? Or maybe you've heard about the pasta parties held the night before many marathons or IRONMAN races. In both cases, they're a little overboard from what's required.

In my early triathlon days, I fell victim to the common misconception that before a race, more carbs equals a good performance. The night before my first triathlon, which was just a 40-minute try-a-tri, I ate an enormous plate of pasta. Later that night, I also ate a giant bowl of cereal because the more carbs the better, right? Then, the morning of the race, I had a big breakfast to "get those carb stores topped up." You can't have too many, or so I thought.

Turns out you can. When I got to the race, I spent my entire transition set-up time in and out of the porta-potty. I had a softball-sized lump in my stomach from the previous night's lasagna. Once I got into the race, and especially during the run, it felt like I was running with the little monster from *Alien* in my belly because the contents were sloshing around.

After the race was over, my stomach was in tatters. I spent the rest of the day on the toilet nursing my sore stomach but thinking that was just the price you pay to be a champion... of a local, fun try-a-tri... with 12 other participants.

The concept of carb-loading is meant to top up your muscle and liver glycogen stores. Your glycogen stores are essentially the energy stores you'll start the race with. Most people have a maximum capacity to store around 2,000 to 2,500 calories worth of muscle glycogen (each gram of carbohydrate equals four calories), so even if you're starting from a completely depleted state (which most people aren't because they're tapering in the few days leading up to a race) it only takes a maximum of 625 grams of carbs to completely top up your glycogen stores.

The average male eats approximately 296 grams of carbs in an average day while the average female eats approximately 225 grams of carbs per day. Without carb-loading, that's already around 1,000 available calories. The graph below shows the average grams of calories stored in the body is 1,100 to 1,600 (graph below is showing grams of glycogen stores and calories stored = grams x 4).

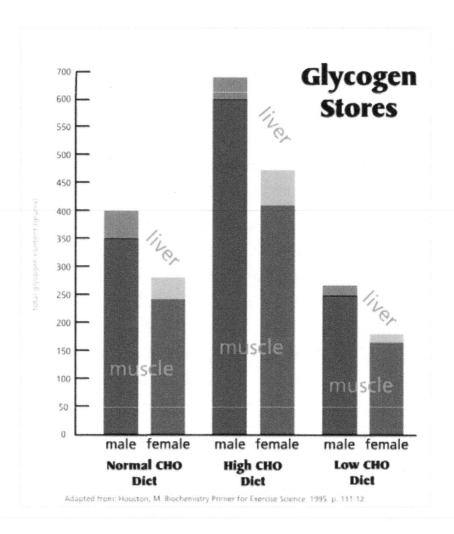

Adapted from: Houston, M. Biochemistry Primer for Exercise Science. 1995. p. 111-12.

Basically, this means you don't need to carb load for breakfast, lunch, dinner, and breakfast again before a race. A slight increase in carbs the day before the race is more than enough to top up muscle and liver glycogen stores and make sure you have a good race, without having to set up camp in the porta-potty.

Later on, we'll discuss how you should plan to eat the day before and the morning of a race.

KETO

I spent the spring and summer of 2019 working with Dr. Dan Plews to test, and hopefully improve, my ability to access fat as fuel. Dan is one of the endurance sport community's leading experts on low carb, high fat performance. With dozens of published papers, he has coached three professional triathletes to sub eight-hour IRONMAN finishes, and he himself was the overall amateur winner and course-record setter at the IRONMAN World Championship in 2018. (You should check out his site endureiq.com if you want to learn about endurance training directly from Dan.)

Dan believes a low carb (100 to 150 grams of carbs per day on average) approach is one of the best ways to improve performance in endurance events that are performed at a steady, sub-maximal pace. But even he does not believe that a sustained keto diet (less than 50 grams of carbs per day) is healthy for endurance athletes. Unfortunately, when I started working with

Dan, a huge number of black and white thinkers could not understand that low carb does not automatically mean keto.

People are primed to place labels on everything and take things to an extreme because it makes things easier. While many studies support a diet that's 85-90% plant-based with whole foods, people go to the extreme and say that 100% strict veganism is the only way to be healthy and any ounce of meat is poison. On the other end of the spectrum, people hear there are benefits to strict carb restriction on a keto diet, so they say fewer carbs is always better and a diet with as low as only 10 grams of carbs per day, every day, for forever, is the only approach.

The reality is the best diet for triathletes doesn't have a name, instead it has principles which can be customized to your unique nutritional needs. Some people do well with fewer carbs and more fat, others with fewer carbs and more protein, some don't do well restricting carbs at all, and some people perform great with 100% plant-based sources of food.

I need to address the keto diet itself not only because it's all the rage at the time of publication, but also because I've been putting out a lot of content on lower carb training lately. Restricting carbs to less than 50 grams per day can be a tool that's part of a lower carb approach to training, but it's not an all-the-time thing. If you want to take a lower carb approach to training, a three-week period of strict carb restriction to less than 50 grams of carbs per day can serve as an adaptation period ONLY. Beyond that, 100 to 150 grams of carbs per day tends to be the sweet spot for most endurance athletes.

This topic fills up many of its own books, including one I may write in the future. If you decide to go down the keto path, just know very few endurance athletes do well on constant extreme carb restriction. Also, the process is far more nuanced than just dramatically restricting carbs, so getting help from qualified sources like Dr. Dan Plews and his courses at endureiq.com is a safer approach than trying to figure it out on your own.

NATURAL FOODS ARE BEST

The recent trend of people moving towards more natural options to eat and drink is a great one. Foods with less artificial junk in them are simply better for the body. Unfortunately, a lot of people have taken this trend to the extreme and believe that if more natural foods are better, then exclusively natural foods, all the time, must be best. This dogmatic approach to natural foods is just as unbalanced as the approach to a strict keto diet or strict veganism, and I believe a more moderate approach is necessary.

Take, for example, our requirements for fluid with electrolytes and calories. Strict natural eaters will typically opt for something like coconut water for fluid, and bananas and dates for their calories. Great in theory, but over the course of an IRONMAN, even these natural items can cause problems.

Coconut water has a sodium to potassium ratio that's very heavily skewed towards potassium, which is the opposite of what is best for athletes. Instead of the desired approximate 4:1 sodium to potassium ratio, coconut water is more like 1:3 sodium to potassium, and that can cause bloating, stalled digestion, cramping, and blood pressure issues. Bananas can cause the same problems due to their high levels of potassium.

Figs and dates were the go-to calorie source for triathletes during the '80s and early '90s, but this presented a risk of problems that could be a little "messy". When we interviewed six-time IRONMAN World Champion Mark Allen on the second episode of the Triathlon Taren Podcast, he told us when he was preparing for his first ever IRONMAN in the '80s, he calculated his calorie requirements for a race to be 32 to 34 dried figs. He only made it to 13 figs before he couldn't stomach eating another, and by that point he'd consumed 40 grams of fiber. Fortunately, it didn't cause Mark any gastrointestinal distress, but it sure could have!

This isn't to say if you eat unprocessed foods more often, that you should abandon those foods immediately and start slugging straight refined sugar. I honestly believe people should eat more whole foods more often. Bring a banana on your long ride, or try making some homemade energy balls. If you're trying a low carb training approach, use natural nut butters. But this doesn't mean that's all you have to eat.

If you choose to incorporate some natural products, monitor how your gut and performance feel when you ingest natural food products during training. If you notice you've got digestive problems, energy issues, cramping, bloating, or anything else undesirable going on, try incorporating a few manufactured sports nutrition products.

Before you say "processed foods are the devil and they'll rot the marrow from inside your bones," just know sports nutrition products are a lot better than they were a decade ago. Many companies are using healthier ingredients. Some energy blocks are now made with organic tapioca syrup instead of straight sugar, a lot of bars contain more whole food ingredients, and gels… well, most gels are still gross, if you ask me.

Are natural foods great? Absolutely! Just try them with caution during exercise and use them in moderation, mixed with some higher quality traditional sports nutrition products.

SPORTS NUTRITION IS BEST

Now, you might be saying, "Taren says natural foods aren't ideal, I'm going to eat nothing but the processed gels, chews, and bars." Again, we don't need to be so staunch toward one approach or the other. Getting on the, sugar, sugar, and more sugar train can also cause problems.

Processed sugars burn very quickly and can cause you to develop a reliance on sugars for any exertion lasting longer than 60 minutes. We don't want you to be one of those runners who absolutely needs their nutrition flask for any run longer than 30 minutes, so if you are using ultra-processed sports nutrition products, try to use them sparingly and not for any workout shorter than 75 minutes.

Refined sugars also drive up your blood glucose more than natural sugars do, so if you use nothing but refined sugars all the time, you could develop indications of Type 2 Diabetes. Sami Inkinen, an amateur triathlon world champion and founder of Virta Health, was one of the fittest people in the world after he won his world championship but he found out he was pre-diabetic due to all the refined sugars he was consuming through his training and race nutrition. Later we'll talk about using carbs, fats and fasted workouts occasionally to achieve a more balanced approach to nutrition which will keep you healthier and allow you to perform well.

Processed sports nutrition is great at the right times, but when mixed with natural food sources, you'll likely see the best results.

FASTED WORKOUTS WILL HELP ME LOSE WEIGHT

I was once on a call with an athlete from Team Trainiac and he said, "I do all my workouts fasted and take no calories during them. I'm seeing great results. I've lost 40 pounds. In other news I've got no energy, sleeping problems, and my performance sucks these days. Any ideas why this could be?"

To which I replied, "Define great results."

Much like the keto diet, veganism, or staunchly avoiding all processed foods, fasted workouts are another approach that has been taken to the extreme. Many triathletes find fasted workouts result in huge weight loss and thus believe it must be a much better approach. Yes, athletes who do fasted workouts will probably lose some weight, but the long-term downsides to fasted workouts are so severe, I rarely recommend strictly fasted workouts.

Hormone imbalances, sleep issues, rebound weight gain, fatigue, and poor immune function are just a few of the long-term consequences of using fasted workouts improperly. These are huge issues than can take years to fix and shedding a few pounds does not outweigh the risks of doing too many fasted workouts.

When I started incorporating lower carb training, many people asked me about fasted workouts, so I did a massive amount of research to create a yes/no flowchart for when fasted workouts can be incorporated and who should (or should not) be doing them.

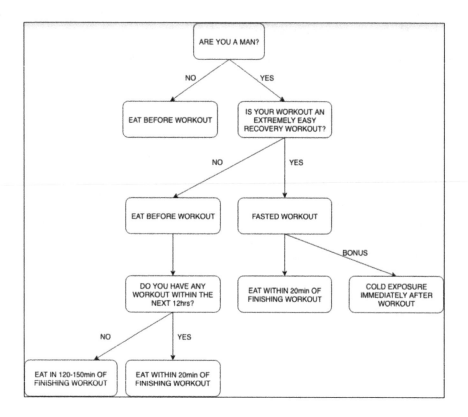

As you can see in the chart, fasted workouts are only a good idea on rare occasions. Research shows, fasted workouts can generally only be used safely by males during extremely short and easy workouts. Females have a bigger risk of developing hormone imbalances from fasted training, and they might *gain weight* doing fasted workouts because of the hormonal impacts on the female body. Fasting before a long or hard workout brings you into the workout on an empty tank and you won't perform as well, so your body won't adapt and get better. You'll also likely chew through your muscle tissue, slowing down your metabolism and leading to long term weight gain. And you'll be placing such a load on your body, it may never be able to recover fully.

Fasted workouts are a tool, but one that should be used very sparingly and only in the right scenario. If you're looking to shed pounds, fat-loss focused training methods like the ones we use on Team Trainiac (lots of low intensity training which burns a lot of fat during exercise, lots of High Intensity Interval Training which burns a lot of fat after exercise, and some strength training which keeps the metabolism high) are a much safer and performance-oriented way to lose weight.

CRAMPING

I've saved the best topic for last! Many, many, many, many, many triathletes believe cramping during exercise is caused by improper nutrition, or a dramatic loss of sodium through sweating. Because cramps are such a big, painful problem, triathletes often take drastic measures seeking the big solution. While nutritional issues play into cramping, often they aren't the real cause.

Sport scientists used to agree cramps were due to nutritional issues, but current studies show this is only in extreme cases of nutritional neglect during exercise. Scientists aren't exactly sure what causes cramping, but best they can figure, cramps are the body's way of trying to shut you down when exercise gets too hard, and your body sees the potential for injury. Your body initiates a cramp to slow you down, in order to reduce the risk of injury. So, the primary cause of cramping is now believed to be pushing harder than you're trained to do.

That's great news because it means to avoid cramps, we just need to get our basic nutrition in check and pace ourselves properly. We take care of the nutrition requirement in this book, and we address pacing in other books in the Foundations series, and on TeamTrainiac.com.

You might be thinking to yourself, "but my sister's friend's cousin said they used salt tabs and pickle juice during a race and it fixed their cramps instantly."

You're right. These items can resolve cramps almost instantly but it's not because the body uses the salt or pickle juice instantly. The fact the cramp goes away almost instantly, proves it's not the salt or the pickle juice that's doing the fixing. If that were the case, it would take 15 to 20 minutes for the cramp to go away because that's how long it would take for the body to digest and process it.

It's believed cramps are caused by a signal from the brain. When you get a cramp, your brain is telling you "This is hard I need to stop, I am giving you a cramp so we can stop," and the strong taste of the salt or the pickle juice seems to give the brain a jostle, snapping it out of that downward spiral almost instantly.

Let's get your basic nutrition in place, get your pacing sorted through your training, and then if you're still experiencing cramps, consider taking a shot of salt or vinegar to reset the brain. It will likely help. Just don't think you've got to move Heaven and Earth, going through sweat rate and sodium loss studies, formulating your exact right personalized nutrition product, in order to avoid cramping.

MATH OF LOW CARB TRIATHLON TRAINING

Before we get into calculating your nutritional requirements, I want to touch on one of the biggest topics that's misunderstood in endurance sports: low carb triathlon training.

I've already discussed how low carb doesn't mean keto when it comes to endurance athletes. But I haven't discussed why a low carb, or rather a "lower carb" approach is something worth considering.

Let's look at some examples to illustrate what I'm getting at. Below are the stats of a typical athlete fuelling exclusively with carbs and eating a typical diet, who is properly carbed-up for a race:

Energy expenditure: 1,000 calories per hour

Available fat as fuel: 0.5g per minute

Maximum ingestible calories during exercise from carbs: 240/hour

Available calories in muscles and liver: 2,000

Now let's look at what happens during a 12-hour IRONMAN race, based on these known values:

Calories burned: 12,000

Calories from fat burned as fuel: 3,240 (0.5g/minute x 720 minutes x 9 calories per gram of fat)

Calories from muscles and liver: 2,000

Calories from ingested carbohydrate fuel: 2,880 (240 calories/hour x 12 hours)

TOTAL AVAILABLE CALORIES: 8,120

CALORIE <u>SHORTFALL</u>: 3,880

This calorie shortfall is why people end up suffering through the marathon, and why an IRONMAN starts getting hard toward the end of bike. When there's a calorie shortfall, you can't just eat more calories to make up for it, because your stomach can only process so much. You also can't magically burn more fat because that requires training ahead of time. So, the body starts chewing into muscle, causing muscular failures and tired, sore muscles that don't want to perform.

Unfortunately, these numbers will not vary and once you get into the race, if you're not able to burn fat as fuel, these numbers remain constant. Your ability to burn fat as fuel is fixed, this won't change during the race. What's pre-loaded into your muscles and liver is fixed, and the only time this number might change is if you're a VERY muscular athlete, in which case you might be able to store an additional 500 calories worth of glycogen. And even with training, it'll be hard to get your stomach to absorb more than 240 calories each hour during exercise. You're almost guaranteed to have rough several last hours of the race, if not outright bonk.

Now, let's look at an example of an athlete who has used a lower carb training method to increase the amount of fat their body can burn each minute.

Energy expenditure: 1,000 calories per hour

Available fat as fuel: 1.2 grams per minute

Maximum ingestible calories during exercise from carbs: 240/hour

Available calories in muscles and liver: 2,000

Let's look at what happens during a 12-hour IRONMAN based on this set of known values:

Calories burned: 12,000

Calories from fat burned as fuel: 7,776 (1.2 grams/minute x 720 minutes x 9 calories per gram of fat)

Calories from muscles and liver: 2,000

Calories from ingested carbohydrate fuel: 2,880 (240 calories/hour x 12 hours)

TOTAL AVAILABLE CALORIES: 12,656

CALORIE SURPLUS: 656

As you can see, being better at accessing fat as fuel has an enormous benefit because someone who is "fat adapted" has access to enough fuel so their performance won't deteriorate in the final third of the race.

The examples above come from Matt Kerr, a friend and triathlete who works with Dr. Dan Plews and Dan's business partner Grant Schofield. Matt went through an 11-week fat adaptation program and increased his fat burning from 0.5 gram/minute to 1.2 gram/minute. In his first IRONMAN, which was just his second triathlon ever, he went 9:20, finishing 11th overall. What's most interesting about his performance is that Matt was sitting in 25th place in the race right up until the final 10 kilometers of the run. During this final 10, Matt simply held his pace, didn't fade, and passed more than a dozen people who were running out of energy.

Getting better at burning fat also isn't new. Pro triathlete Sarah True told me her coach often gets her to do long, low intensity rides without carbs to be able to access more fat. One day when I was lucky enough to ride with two-time World Champion Patrick Lange, I started taking calories at 90 minutes into the ride. He scoffed at me and said, "What are you doing? You don't take sugar on an easy ride until at least three hours in! You have to be able to fuel off fats."

In fact, if you were to test all the pros and elite amateurs in a race of four hours or longer, you'd see that just about every single one of them has an increased ability to burn fat as fuel. This is because one of the main ways you can increase your ability to burn fat is by training a lot... A LOT. Pro triathletes who train upward of 35 hours per week will typically have an increased ability to burn fat simply because of the large training volumes they do.

DISCLAIMER: DO NOT start immediately doing all rides without sugars. It takes time to build up to what Patrick Lange and I talked about on the ride.

Fortunately, we amateurs don't have to train 35 hours a week to increase our ability to burn fat. We can accomplish the same thing by making some small tweaks to our diet. In fact, when we had another partner of Dr. Dan Plews, Dr. Paul Laursen, on the

Triathlon Taren Podcast, he said they believe a triathlete can get the effect of a 25-hour training week in just 15 hours with the right approach to nutrition.

Burning more fat as fuel to enhance performance isn't a new concept; what is new is the extremes to which it's been taken. Notice how above I used the words *"Small tweaks to our diet"* and not *"Massive overhaul of everything you've been told about nutrition to become a metabolically efficient FAT BURNING MACHINE!"*? That's because while the second phrase sounds sexier, it's unnecessary, unsafe, and not applicable to a lot of amateur athletes. No, you don't have to stuff your cycling jersey pockets with bacon to accomplish what Matt Kerr did, but you do need to time and approach your nutrition slightly differently than you probably are right now.

I'll discuss some of the small things you can change to effectively burn more fat later, in the section called "Periodize Your Nutrition". For now, just know there's some validity to becoming better at using fat as fuel, and this means a slight decrease in carbs, a slight change in some of your workouts, and some temporary diet changes -- but NOT a complete lifestyle overhaul to become a so-called FAT BURNING MACHINE!

CHAPTER 4

BEFORE YOUR RACE

There's a TV commercial in Canada where a young, professional NHL hockey player is drinking a pre-workout sports drink, an all-natural greens supplement, as he gets ready for a game. He looks across the dressing room and, sitting at a dinner table, are three old legendary hockey players wearing their full hockey gear, scarfing down massive plates of pasta right before the game. The modern-day hockey player says, "Guys, a lot has changed since your days." And the grizzled veterans keep inhaling more pasta.

It used to be thought that if you wanted to perform well for anything, no matter how long or short the competition, you had to carb load with pasta. You'd definitely load up the day before the event, maybe the morning of the event, and, if you were really serious, right before the event. Science now tells us this isn't necessary or even helpful, but this newer scientific knowledge has not made its way into the general culture of endurance sports. I learned this lesson the hard way very early on (see my story earlier in the book of my massive carb load the night before and morning of my very first, 40-minute try-a-tri race, which left my guts in tatters).

The need for pre-event carb loading still seems to be the enduring belief in endurance sports, despite a lot of basic knowledge that has made its way to a lot of other sports. Heck, in some ways, it HAS penetrated the culture of our sport; you don't carb load the night before every workout do you? And you still seem to have a lot of good workouts, right? Yet, come race day, triathletes get all worked up and try to pump themselves full of carbs in hopes it'll turn them into The Hulk.

So, what's the right approach that gets you as Hulk-like as possible without the downsides that come with overloading the body with carbs? Well, it's much easier and more moderate than you might think.

PRE-RACE DAY EATING

As I mentioned before, the maximum amount of glycogen you can store in your muscles and liver is likely somewhere between 2,000 and 2,500 calories. That is what you need to top up before your race. However, you aren't ever starting with zero calories of stored energy in your muscles and your liver; most people's glycogen stores are at least 1,200 calories while the average person already has the 2,000 calories stored up, day-to-day.[1] So even if you didn't change your diet in the days leading up to a race, you'll likely be able to perform. We just want to make sure you're able to perform to the best of your ability for the entire race.

All you need to do in the days leading up to the race is to *slightly* increase the carbohydrates you consume. You'll need to do this for two days for a half-IRONMAN or IRONMAN, and just one day for a Sprint or Olympic distance triathlon.

When I say, "increase the carbohydrates slightly," I mean you can eat roughly 5 to 10% more than you typically would, and just eat 10% more of your typical calories from carbohydrates. For example, in the months leading up to Challenge Roth (my first full IRONMAN-distance race), I averaged 130 grams of carbs per day. In the two days prior to the race, I increased my daily carbohydrate consumption to just 200 grams of carbs; 70 grams of carbs is a couple of sweet potatoes, four slices of bread, or a big bowl of oatmeal.

So, don't go and eat carbs upon carbs upon carbs, thinking more is better. Anything more than just a slightly greater amount of carb intake than usual, and you're not doing yourself

---

[1] https://www.ncbi.nlm.nih.gov/pmc/articles/PMC6019055/

any favors, you're just adding more food to your digestive tract that could cause digestive issues during the race.

Finally, there are some foods you should avoid in the days before a race to set yourself up for success. Stay away from foods that could back you up, send you racing to the toilet, or cause general digestive stress.

Foods you know back you up might prevent you from getting everything out of your digestive tract before the race; you never want half-digested food bouncing around in your body during the race. Cheese, unripe bananas, white bread, and fast food/fried foods often get people bunged up, so it's best to avoid them in the several days prior to a race.

Conversely, you also don't want to be unnaturally cleaned out, having to spend a lot of time in a porta-potty prior to the race. If there are foods that traditionally send you running to the toilet, it's best to avoid them and don't increase the amount of fiber you eat in the days leading up to a race.

Lastly, here's a list of FODMAP foods that often cause digestive issues. Review this list and if you don't eat them often, or if you know they have caused you issues in the past, it'll be best to avoid them close to the race. Common FODMAPS:

- **Fruits:** Apples, applesauce, apricots, blackberries, cherries, canned fruit, dates, figs, pears, peaches, watermelon

- **Sweeteners:** Fructose, honey, high fructose corn syrup, xylitol, mannitol, maltitol, sorbitol

- **Dairy products:** Milk (from cows, goats and sheep), ice cream, most yogurts, sour cream, soft and fresh cheeses (cottage, ricotta, etc.) and whey protein

- **Vegetables:** Artichokes, asparagus, broccoli, beets, Brussels sprouts, cabbage, cauliflower, garlic, mushrooms, okra, onions, peas, shallots

- **Legumes:** Beans, chickpeas, lentils, red kidney beans, soybeans

- **Wheat:** Bread, pasta, breakfast cereals, tortillas, waffles, pancakes, crackers, biscuits

- **Other grains:** Barley and rye

- **Beverages:** Beer, fortified wines, soft drinks (high-fructose corn syrup), milk, alternative "milks" such as soy, fruit juices

Stick to eating foods you know you digest easily, eat just a tad more, and increase your carbs only slightly in the one or two days leading up to the race. Do that, and you'll be set to perform well and likely not have digestive issues on race day.

PRE-RACE DAY FLUIDS

Just as you want to have your calorie and carbohydrate levels properly topped up by the time you head to bed the night before the race, you want to do the same thing with your fluids and electrolytes.

Making sure you're properly hydrated with enough electrolytes will reduce the likelihood of cramping or encountering blood pressure issues. Fortunately, getting yourself hydrated in the days leading up to the race is very easy.

Two days out from your race, have a water bottle with a no-calorie electrolyte supplement like Nuun, UCAN Electrolytes, or Base Electrolyte Salt. Sip this throughout the day. Also be sure to have a big glass of water upon waking, and water with dinner.

This is all most athletes need to do to get their fluid and electrolyte levels topped-up prior to a race.

If you've eaten a slightly higher amount of carbs and kept yourself hydrated in the days leading up to a race, your work is basically done. Your glycogen levels will be topped up, you'll be hydrated, and your sodium levels will be ready. Race morning will be easy for you. Here's a suggested schedule for your race morning.

4 HOURS PRIOR TO RACE START

You'll want to set your alarm exactly four hours prior to the race start. Even if your race is starting at 6:30am you'll want to get up four hours prior to the race to eat your race morning breakfast. By eating your race morning breakfast four hours prior to the race start, the breakfast food will be cleared from your stomach but not yet waiting to be eliminated, so you won't have any food material jostling around during the race.

This breakfast does not need to be big, nor does it have to be anything in particular. Many athletes have a hard time eating the morning of a race due to nerves. Two-time world champion Mirinda Carfrae says she eats whatever she can get down. Pro triathlete Andy Potts eats sugary muffins because they're tasty. Essentially, you want a small carb-based meal of no more than 300 to 400 calories.

We also want the race day breakfast to follow the guidelines we mentioned in the previous chapter: low in fiber, no dairy, nothing that will upset your stomach. If you want the best breakfast possible, you'll want to select a complex carbohydrate which will provide the longest lasting energy without a big blood sugar spike and a crash over the following several hours. Examples of good race day breakfasts are:

- Two small pieces of whole grain or sprouted toast with nut butter, jam, or honey
- Whole grain cereal with a dairy-free milk

- Sweet potatoes
- Leftover pasta (but watch the serving size, it's very easy to over-serve dense pasta)
- My personal favorite (because it's such a slow digesting source of energy) is plain, natural, slow-cooked oats with UCAN SuperStarch powder mixed in
- UCAN SuperStarch bars

Don't bother drinking fluids to hydrate at breakfast as that will come later. You can have coffee if you want as it won't hurt performance.

If you're racing in a climate that's far hotter than where you normally train, you may want to have a hyper-hydrator that provides you with a huge serving of electrolytes. Nuun, Skratch, and Osmo make good preload hydration products that can be mixed at breakfast with just a half cup of water.

BETWEEN BREAKFAST AND RACE

At this point, just about everything you need to do is done. There's just one last thing I like to do after breakfast and between the race for nutrition.

While your hydration levels are likely full at this point and you don't need much more in the way of fluids or electrolytes, some people get a dry mouth, and some people (like me) have nervous energy before a race.

To keep your hands busy and your mouth lubricated, so you feel comfortable and relaxed before the race, fill a small disposable bottle with 8-12 ounces of a light electrolyte drink. You're looking for something without any calories but with a small amount of electrolytes, something like a Nuun, Base Salt, or UCAN electrolytes.

Sip this bottle whenever you want to but don't feel as though you must finish it. The reason I recommend a disposable bottle is so you can sip the bottle right up until it's time to start the process of warming up, and you can then ditch the bottle in the garbage or with a race volunteer.

Congratulations, you're now ready to race!

CHAPTER 5

SCHEDULE YOUR RACE NUTRITION

STEP 1: CALCULATE YOUR CALORIES BURNED

The first step in getting your race nutrition sorted is to calculate the number of calories you'll be burning during the race. The main variables that impact this are your weight and your pace; the heavier you are, the more calories you'll burn. Likewise, the faster you're going, the more calories you'll burn. There are some other variables which effect how many calories you're burning (such as how efficiently you're swimming, biking, or running, and your history of training), but for the purposes of your race nutrition calculation, using your weight and your pace will get us close enough.

ENERGY EXPENDITURE VALUES FOR DIFFERENT EXERCISE ACTIVITIES

Activity (Energy Expenditure Value)	cal./min./lb.
Swimming (50 yards/minute):	0.06
Swimming (75 yards/minute):	0.08
Cycling (10 miles per hour):	0.06
Cycling (15 miles per hour):	0.08
Cycling (17.5 miles per hour):	0.09
Cycling (>20 miles per hour):	0.12
Running (5.5 minute/mile):	0.13
Running (6 minute/mile):	0.11
Running (7 minute/mile):	0.10
Running (8 minute/mile):	0.09
Running (9 minute/mile):	0.09
Running (11.5 minute/mile):	0.06

CREDIT: *The Performance Zone* by John Ivy, PhD and Robert Portman, PhD

Above is a table of how many calories you'll burn based on weight and pace. You can use this table to calculate it manually or go to triathlontaren.com/nutritionfoundations to download a free calculator that you can use to calculate your requirement automatically. It will calculate your calories burned and calories required for all distances of triathlon (and all your training) in just five seconds.

STEP 2: CALCULATE 25% OF YOUR CALORIES BURNED

The next step in determining your race nutrition strategy is to figure out how many calories you need to replace, based on how many calories you'll burn. To get this number, we'll simply multiply the calories you burn by 0.25 to determine 25% of your burned calories.

Sharp readers will note I previously mentioned athletes can consume a maximum of about 60 grams of carbs per hour. An athlete going all-out might burn as many as 1,000 calories per hour, 25% of which is 250 calories to consume to fuel that effort AND coincidentally 60 grams of carbs per hour equals 240 calories, basically exactly as much as you want to replace.

Rather than just saying athletes can absorb 50 to 60 grams of carbs per hour and they should take as much as possible, we want to customize our nutrition with this 25% of calories burned rule. So, take your result from Step 1 and multiply that by 0.25.

STEP 3: SELECT YOUR RACE NUTRITION

Whether you're a traditional, carb-based triathlete or you've transitioned to more of a lower carb training approach, race nutrition should still be based on carbs. Both studies and anecdotal accounts support the best performance happens when athletes train with a lower amount of carbohydrates and race using a more traditional high carbohydrate approach. This method is like supercharging your performance because you've trained to perform well without many carbs in the system, then you give your body easy access to carbs and get both a high amount of fat as fuel AND easy to access carbohydrates.

I personally saw this exact approach work well for me at Challenge Roth in 2019. Leading up to the race, a "high" carbohydrate training session might only have 40 grams of carbohydrates, while entire days averaged only 130 grams of carbs. Then, on race day, I had 45 grams of carbs in the morning via oatmeal and UCAN SuperStarch, and 20 grams of carbs many times throughout the day totalling 500 grams of carbohydrates throughout the entire race. I felt great and dare I say the race felt easy... until the final 15 kilometers where I had to gut out some dark mental times, but I still held perfect 5-minute kilometers throughout the entire marathon.

Once you've calculated your required calories, and you've got a race nutrition schedule planned (which we'll do in just a second), what you choose to use as a source of calories is easy. Simply select whatever carbs you like the taste of; your stomach is so compromised on race day, if you get the calories and scheduling right, the specifics of what to consume isn't critical.

I've had good success with Clif Blocks, primarily on the bike because they're maltodextrin-based which is easy to digest (but can leave you feeling dry afterwards because this product requires more fluid for the body to process). I mix the blocks with Picky Bars just to keep a settled stomach, and get some whole foods. Then, on the run I switch to Coke to get the one-two punch of caffeine and sugar while not forcing my body to try to digest solids. That said, multi-time IRONMAN winner Lucy Charles-Barclay eats Snickers bars during her races. Really, whatever tastes good is going to be the best for your stomach, which will result in you sticking to your required calories and race nutrition plan.

STEP 4: SCHEDULE YOUR RACE NUTRITION

Your next step is to figure out the schedule for your race nutrition. What follows may sound complicated so the custom race nutrition calculator here, at triathlontaren.com/nutritionfoundations, will not only do the calorie requirements calculation for you, but it will also give you a nutrition schedule during a race customized based on what your chosen nutrition products are.

There are a couple of benefits to creating a race nutrition schedule ahead of time, as opposed to just figuring it out, on the fly, on race day.

First, a schedule will get incorporated into your race plan thus making nutrition a priority. It's easy to think about race nutrition as an afterthought if you haven't worked out a strict schedule. Simply saying, "I need about 700 calories, which is seven gels, so I'll just stuff them in my pocket and take them as I need" is setting yourself up for failure because there are a lot of things to think about during the race, and if your race nutrition isn't pre-determined beforehand, it's unlikely it will be well-executed during the race.

Second, a strict race nutrition schedule doses your calories and fluid evenly so your stomach never has too much or too little to digest. Sticking to an evenly distributed schedule for your nutrition will make it easier for your stomach to digest small amounts of nutrition as you go.

To figure out your race nutrition schedule, start by going back to the number of calories you worked out that you'll have to replace from Step 2. You want to then create a race nutrition plan that is as follows:

Sprint/Olympic/70.3 Plan	IRONMAN Plan
1. 20 minutes before race	20 minutes before race
2. 10 minutes into bike	T1
3. Regular intervals	Regular intervals
4. 10 minutes before T2	10 minutes before T2
5. 10 minutes after T2	10 minutes after T2
6. Regular intervals	Regular intervals
7. 10 minutes before finish line	10 minutes before finish line

Where the math comes in is figuring out what your regular intervals are for bike and run nutrition. To do this, you'll use the formula below (or, to get the schedule calculated for you, just go to triathlontaren.com/nutritionfoundations).

Here's how to do the calculation for a Sprint, Olympic, or 70.3:

1. X-number of calories per serving of your chosen race nutrition (always check the package for this number)

2. Add up known calorie intervals: 20 minutes before race + 10 minutes into bike + 10 minutes prior to T2 + 10 minutes after T2 + 10 minutes before end of race

3. Subtract the total from step 2 from your target number of calories

4. Divide the remaining calories by the number of calories of your chosen race nutrition from step 1

5. Round the number from step 4 to the nearest number

6. Subtract swim time + 40 from total race time

7. Divide the figure from step 6 by the figure from step 5

To illustrate an example schedule, let's use a five-hour half-IRONMAN, with a 35-minute swim, 1,000 required calories, and let's assume your chosen race nutrition product features 80 calories per serving (this is the ideal serving size because it's a small amount of foods that's easy for your stomach to digest).

1. Number of calories per serving of your chosen race nutrition: <u>80 calories</u>

2. Add up known calorie intervals: 5 feeding times x 80 calories = <u>400 calories</u>

3. Subtract the total from step 2 from your target number of calories: 1,000 calories - 400 calories = <u>600 remaining calories</u>

4. Divide the remaining calories by the number of calories in your chosen race nutrition from step 1: 600 remaining calories / 80 calories = <u>7.5</u>

5. Round the number from step 4 to the nearest number: 7.5 rounds to = <u>8 feeding times</u>

6. Subtract swim time + 40 from total race time: 300 minutes total race time - 35-minute swim - 40 minutes = <u>225 remaining feeding minutes</u>

7. Divide the figure from step 6 by the figure from step 5: 225 minutes / 8 feeds = <u>28-minute feeding interval</u>

Now that we have those numbers, we can create a mock race nutrition schedule to make sure the schedule provides us with our target required calories:

1. 20 minutes before race   80 calories

2. 10 minutes into bike   80 calories

3. 28 minutes later   80 calories

4. 28 minutes later   80 calories

5. 28 minutes later   80 calories

6. 28 minutes later   80 calories

7. 10 minutes before T2   80 calories

8. 10 minutes after T2   80 calories

9. 28 minutes later   80 calories

10. 28 minutes later   80 calories

11. 10 minutes before finish line   80 calories

TOTAL: 960 calories

You can see the calculation gets us roughly the right number of calories you'll require to perform well in the race. At this point, you've taken in enough calories to make sure you can perform well while not overloading your stomach, and you've spaced out the feedings far enough to allow your stomach time to digest the calories.

You'll also probably notice the calculation is 40 calories short of the target 1,000 calories. This is not a big deal; 5 to 7% one way or the other isn't a deal breaker. However, if your calories and schedule are off the target significantly, you'll want to recheck your calculations.

Fuel scheduling for an IRONMAN-distance race is very similar with one adjustment to the calculation. In an IRONMAN, we add a liquid carbohydrate drink in Transition 1 before getting on the bike. This addition of a calorie feed at this point in your race ensures you get on the bike at least at a neutral caloric level. An IRONMAN race is a gruelling event, so we want to make sure at no point are we depleting our caloric or energy stores more than necessary. The only other difference in the calculation is that in step 6, you'll subtract 30 minutes from the total race time instead of 40 minutes.

Let's illustrate an example schedule using an 11-hour IRONMAN with a 75-minute swim, 1950 required calories, and a nutrition product featuring 80 calories per serving (again, this is the ideal serving size because it's a small amount of food that's easy for your stomach to digest).

1. Number of calories per serving in your chosen race nutrition: <u>80 calories</u>

2. Add up known calorie intervals: 5 feeding times x 80 calories = <u>400 calories</u>

3. Subtract the total from step 2 from your target number of calories: 1,950 calories - 400 calories = <u>1,550 remaining calories</u>

4. Divide the remaining calories by the number of calories in your chosen race nutrition from step 1: 1,550 remaining calories / 80 calories = <u>19.375</u>

5. Round the number from step 4 to the nearest number: 19.375 rounds to = <u>19 feeding times</u>

6. Subtract swim time + 30 from total race time: 660 minutes total race time - 75-minute swim - 30 minutes = <u>555 remaining feeding minutes</u>

7. Divide the figure from step 6 by the figure from step 5: 555 minutes / 19 feeds = <u>29-minute feeding interval</u>

And again, we can create a mock race nutrition schedule to make sure we've got our target required calories:

1. 20 minutes before race   80 calories

2. Transition 1   80 calories

3. 29 minutes later   80 calories

4. 29 minutes later   80 calories

5. 29 minutes later   80 calories

6. 29 minutes later   80 calories

7. 29 minutes later   80 calories

8. 29 minutes later   80 calories

9. 29 minutes later   80 calories

10. 29 minutes later   80 calories

11. 29 minutes later   80 calories

12. 29 minutes later   80 calories

13. 29 minutes later   80 calories

14. 29 minutes later   80 calories

15. 10 minutes before T2   80 calories

16. 10 minutes after T2   80 calories

17. 29 minutes later   80 calories

18. 29 minutes later   80 calories

19. 29 minutes later   80 calories

20. 29 minutes later   80 calories

21. 29 minutes later   80 calories

22. 29 minutes later   80 calories

23. 29 minutes later   80 calories

24. 10 minutes before finish line   80 calories

TOTAL: 1,920 calories

Notice, in both versions of the schedule, the calculations work out so that you're pretty close to your calculated required calories.

Of course, this nutrition schedule is what will theoretically happen in a perfect environment. But races aren't perfect environments. Aid stations are at irregular intervals, your stomach might go south on you, or the race day conditions might be hotter or colder than where you trained. All these possible issues will be addressed in a later chapter. But now you've got your baseline nutrition plan, which will put you miles ahead of your competition, literally.

FLUIDS

It's a more complicated process to determine your fluid consumption requirement level ahead of time. Factors like exercise intensity, altitude, air temperature, humidity, and your sweat rate cause your fluid loss (and thus your fluid requirements) to vary wildly from workout to workout, and race to race.

Unfortunately, there's no easy calculation for fluid requirements; you could be a light but salty sweater like me, or you could be a heavy sweater like IRONMAN World Champion Chris McCormack and pro triathlete Emma Pallant. Of course, if you want to really dial in your fluid plan, the first place to start would be to perform a sweat test like the pros do. However, while getting the fluid requirements precisely right is critical for the professionals, for us amateur triathletes, I can simplify things with an easy and broadly applicable fluid approach that will work for most people.

"CALORIES IN YOUR POCKET, FLUIDS IN YOUR BOTTLE"

The saying, "Calories in your pocket and fluids in your bottle," is common when discussing race nutrition for cycling or triathlon. It means athletes should separate their calories from their fluids and electrolytes; essentially relying on things like blocks, gels, bars, and real food for the most calories, and using plain water or a light electrolyte drink with minimal or no calories for hydration.

Many new triathletes, overwhelmed with all of these calculations, undoubtedly hear about some of the all-in-one fluid and calorie solutions like Tailwind, Heed, or Infinite. Or maybe they've watched Lionel Sanders discuss his race nutrition for IRONMAN Kona 2018 where he used strictly Gatorade and water.

While some people do have success with these all-in-one race nutrition products, science (and post-race stories from countless athletes) show they often cause more problems than they solve.

The premise behind these all-in-one nutritional solutions is you get your fluids, electrolytes, and easy-to-access carbohydrate calories from just one liquid. Stanford researcher and founder of Osmo Nutrition, Dr. Stacey Sims, explains when liquid drinks are full of the required sugars, the body forces water away from your blood and muscles and into the GI tract to effectively digest it. In other words, the drink ends up somewhat dehydrating you.

Another issue with these all-in-one solutions is they don't allow you to customize your fluids independent of your calories. Calorie requirements, as based on the calculations from the previous chapters, will be a pretty stable number from race to race but fluid requirements are not.

Let's say you're using an all-in-one sports nutrition product in an extremely hot weather race which requires you to consume more fluids. This is also going to jack up your consumed calories beyond what you need or can digest, leading to an unpleasant gut situation. Or let's say the opposite happens and you're having stomach issues with your fluid and are unable to consume fluids other than straight water. If you're using an all-in-one, you'll also be eliminating your source of calories.

Beyond that, I've heard many other horror stories from athletes who used all-in-one nutrition products than I have from other race nutrition approaches. I've probably had more than a dozen athletes tell me that while using an all-in-one, they developed cramps, had stomach issues, or faded towards the end of the bike and struggled through the whole run.

For these reasons, we recommend you follow the calorie schedule we laid out in previous chapters and get your calories from sources like gels, chews, bars, or natural food. To achieve the proper balance of fluids, electrolytes, and hydration, we recommend water or a light electrolyte drink without many calories. Products like Skratch, Osmo, and SOS have a good proportion of electrolytes and just enough carbohydrates to make them easily absorbable. If you're following a strict low carb approach for some workouts and don't want any sugar whatsoever, you can consider products like UCAN electrolytes, Nuun, or water with a straight electrolyte like Base Electrolyte Salt.

HOW MUCH IS ENOUGH?

As I previously mentioned, if you really want to dial in how much fluid you need to replace in a race, you could start with a sweat test in a lab but that's not practical (or necessary) for most athletes. Constant sweat rate testing also isn't flexible as an athlete's sweat rate changes across race conditions and throughout the season as an athlete gets more fit.

We suggest simplifying fluid intake using a very simple process which will allow you to make sure you're adequately hydrated for almost any race. It doesn't require testing or calculations, just the ability to stick to a schedule and feel out your body.

A general rule of thumb for how much an athlete should drink during intense endurance exercise is one large 26-ounce bottle of fluid every hour. But this might be a little too much or not quite enough depending on all the factors we outlined above. So, here's the easy three step process we recommend to nail down your fluid intake:

Step 1: For all of your workouts, fill up the equivalent of one 26-ounce bottle of fluid for every hour you plan to train.

Step 2: Take a large sip from a bottle every 5 minutes, learning how large a sip you need to take to consume one bottle per hour.

Step 3: Pay attention to the signals your body gives you with respect to your hydration levels. If you're burping or feel like liquid is sloshing around in your stomach, take smaller or less frequent sips. If you feel thirsty or consistently feel fatigued as the workout goes on, take larger or more frequent sips

That's it. Honest! By repeating this process day after day, training session after training session, you'll start to develop a natural sense of how much fluid to take in. It'll become like driving where you won't really think about it very much and you'll just start drinking as your body requires it.

This process can also be your default race hydration strategy. Regardless of the race altitude, temperature, or intensity, you can always start a race with the measurement of one bottle per hour of effort, then if you've done the training to develop your sense of how much fluid is enough, you'll automatically start dialling in your hydration intake on race day.

STRAIGHT WATER IN ONE BOTTLE

While the above strategy can work flawlessly in training, it can sometimes break down on race day when we factor in nerves and the extended high energy output during a race. Occasionally, even if you've done the three-step fluid intake training protocol we've detailed, you'll end up with a bit of stomach distress during a race. This is common and we have a simple solution.

Leading into Challenge Roth 2019, I was speaking with Dr. Dan Plews about my nutrition strategy. He said I should keep one bottle of straight water with me and if my stomach started to feel funny, I should switch from my electrolyte solution to the water while keeping up my calorie intake. Then, when my stomach felt better, switch back to electrolytes. Dan's belief was the water changes the osmolality in your stomach and helps settle it down.

I'd never really had a problem with fluid intake in previous races, but during Challenge Roth I started to feel a little funny in my stomach during the bike. As per Plews's instruction, I switched to the water and within 10 minutes, my stomach felt perfect again. Later, during the run, the same thing happened so I switched from Coke to water for a couple of aid stations and once again, my stomach felt better. The result of the race was a 9:41 in my first attempt at the full IRONMAN distance, with zero power drop towards the end of the bike and I did not fall off my target 5 minute/kilometer run pace for the entire 42.2 kilometers.

You might be wondering how you're going to carry another water bottle without adding too much weight to your bike or ruining the aerodynamics. I worried about this too.

I don't think this backup water strategy is necessary for Sprint and Olympic distance races as these races tend to be short and painful anyway, and they're over quickly, so any stomach discomfort is likely to be temporary.

For a half-IRONMAN, the backup water bottle can be added to a single water bottle holder behind the seat (go with a 45-degree angle model as it's more aerodynamic) or in between the aerobars. These options don't affect the aerodynamics of the bike and the additional pound of weight is a small price to pay for potentially avoiding hours of poor performance due to stomach discomfort.

For a full IRONMAN-distance race, this backup water bottle strategy is critical as even the slightest bit of discomfort could result in massive time consequences. From a weight standpoint, the additional bottle is going to be a small drop in the bucket of the gels, chews, bars, and flat repair kits you'll strap onto your bike for the race. Don't worry about the weight. As far as aerodynamics are concerned, the between-the-aerobars option and the behind-the-seat option are good ways to store a bottle without a big impact.

45-degree, seat-mounted bottle cage

Aerobar bottle cage

SOLIDS vs. LIQUIDS

A discussion about fluid intake wouldn't be complete if we didn't discuss whether you should take solids (gels, chews, and bars) or liquids. There's some good science out there which, in my experience, successfully guides us into a well-rounded nutrition plan.

In a study titled "Oxidation of solid versus liquid CHO sources during exercise"[2] researchers found that while cycling, solid foods such as gels and bars were combusted just as well as liquids. Another study titled "Exercise performance as a

---

[2] https://www.ncbi.nlm.nih.gov/pubmed/20404762

function of semi-solid and liquid carbohydrate feedings during prolonged exercise"[3] found once running was included in a test, liquids were absorbed better than solids.

In my experience, the best performances I've experienced in longer distance events have come when I took my calories from gels, chews, and bars on the bike (fluids were of course from fluids), then switched over to two separate liquids (one for calories and one for hydration) on the run.

At the end of this book, I'll provide examples of the exact race nutrition schedules and products I've used successfully in the past.

---

[3] https://www.ncbi.nlm.nih.gov/pubmed/7751072

CHAPTER 6

DIAL IN YOUR NUTRITION

Earlier, we talked about how lowering your carbohydrate intake during certain workouts can increase your ability to access fat as fuel. This has enormous benefits for longer distance events such as half-IRONMAN and IRONMAN distance events (Sprint and Olympic racers won't see nearly as much benefit because muscle and liver glycogen, plus a little carbohydrate intake during the race, will be more than enough fuel).

When athletes hear "low carb approach" they typically think it's a complete diet change featuring nothing but avocados, butter coffees, bacon, and steak with asparagus. This is much more extreme than is needed to get the benefits of a lower carb approach to training.

Before I ever considered myself a "low carb athlete," I had started reducing the amount of refined carbohydrates in my diet. Also, due to my dad being diagnosed with celiac disease and my personal testing showing gluten might be a problem for me as well, I had been eating a gluten-free diet. But I really wouldn't have considered what I ate to be a "low carb" diet. Yet, when I did a fat oxidation test, the results showed I was already capable of burning 1.2g of fat per minute, which is nearly pro level.

In this chapter, I'm going to tell you how to make small changes to your daily eating and workout nutrition which will have a significant impact on your race results without forcing you to stuff avocados in your jersey before you go for a ride. With these changes, and some proper training, you may be able to get the benefits of a 25-hour training week in just 15 hours of training.

PERIODIZE WHAT YOU EAT

A well-structured training plan changes throughout the year, progressing from off-season, to base fitness building season, to strength and speed building season, to race season. Each season has different types of workouts and different desired outcomes; off-season and base building season feature shorter less intense workouts and more weight training to build a foundation of fitness, while race season typically features less (if any) weightlifting and longer intense intervals at or above race pace.

For elite athletes and coaches, this periodization and manipulation of workouts throughout the year has been common knowledge for a long time. But, the concept of periodizing nutrition throughout the year or even within a week hasn't really entered the wider culture of endurance performance. Athletes tend to eat the same thing, at the same time, during all days and all workouts, reducing the likelihood of improving their ability to burn fat as fuel.

I'm not suggesting a complete restructuring of everything you thought you knew about nutrition, as some online blog posts and pundits would lead you to believe. The mindset shift is as simple as matching workout mindset to the mindset you have regarding your nutrition. Athletes already change up their workouts depending on the intention of the workout: some workouts are long and easy to build endurance, while other workouts are short and intense to build speed. Likewise, some of your daily nutritional choices should be to encourage fat oxidizing improvements, while other choices should be to jack yourself up with carbs for intense efforts.

CARB REDUCTION

One of the first changes you can make to improve your ability to burn fat is to reduce the amount of refined carbohydrates in your diet. Of all the changes I'm going to suggest, this will likely be the most drastic change most people make.

I'm not going to mandate that you HAVE TO completely eliminate refined carbohydrates from your diet. Instead, a good diet you can stick to is better than a diet so perfect and strict that it gets abandoned. So, an 80/20, or 90/10, or 95/5 healthy versus indulgent diet is certainly enough to make significant changes in your overall health, your appearance, and your performance.

I'm not a huge believer in eating SUPER clean six days a week then having one big cheat day. I was in my early 20s when I originally got healthier, losing 55 pounds, going from 215 pounds down to 160 pounds. During that time, I ate militantly clean for six days then ate like a total idiot every Saturday. This eating pattern was so unrealistically restrictive that I'd spend six days fantasizing about the junk food I was going to eat on Saturday, then on Saturday I'd ravenously scarf down endless junk food all day long, like donuts, gummy candies, sugary cereal, and fast food. This approach created negative associations for me with healthy food; food was either bland, boring, and a punishment, or it was so mouth-wateringly unhealthy that it was lustful. Food shouldn't be a punishment or an object of desire.

A better approach would have been something more like a 90/10 approach, where 90% of the foods I ate on a daily basis would be totally healthy and 10% would be a little indulgent. Within that 10% of indulgent foods, you can make some small changes to keep them as a nice treat, while not pumping total junk into your body.

For example, in my diet now, the vast majority of my days will feature primarily good, clean, "whole" foods but I'll eat an entire pizza on the weekend or go out for a savory Vietnamese meal at our favorite local spot. I'll also have some 90% dark chocolate after dinner, and I'll have a tasty low carb bar. These treats satiate my need for unhealthy foods enough to make me feel like I'm never on a diet.

Here are some simple eliminations or swaps you can make to reduce your intake of refined carbs:

- Swap cereal for natural oats
- Swap milk in coffee for full fat cream
- Swap pasta for zucchini noodles or low carb pasta
- Greatly reduce bread or swap for a low carb version
- Swap starchy carbs for salads on the side of your main dish
- Swap carb-based snack bars for low carb options like low carb bars, sugar-free nut butters, or natural meat snacks like natural/organic pepperoni or jerky (just check the ingredients to make sure they're not full of sugar or other yucky additives)
- When choosing fruits, try to stick to ones that don't jack up your blood sugar too much, like apples, green bananas, or berries

- Eliminate pop and fruit juices, instead drink naturally flavored carbonated water

- Try not to drink your calories

If you're taking the low carb approach to triathlon training seriously, your average daily carb intake on most days should land between 100 to 150 grams of carbs per day. You can track this easily and relatively accurately with an app like Senza.

MINIMAL SUGARS FOR ENDURANCE EFFORTS

Have you ever gone on a cardio machine at a big gym and looked at the console that featured a graphic of heart rate training zones? All these graphics look the same: maximum heart rate declines as people get older, and they indicate the fat burning zone is at a low heart rate. Those graphics, while inaccurate from person to person, are correct in their generalization that it's easier to burn fat at lower heart rates.

However, carbohydrates are typically the preferred source of fuel for people with a standard diet, so if you eat a bunch of carbs before a workout, you'll be shutting down your ability to burn fat as fuel, no matter how low your heart rate is. Eat carbs before every single workout, day after day, and you won't be able to burn fat as fuel; you'll be that athlete who runs out of gas part way through a race.

On TeamTrainiac.com, we have four non-negotiable workouts every week: an endurance focused swim, and endurance focused bike, an endurance focused run, and a strength training session. Triathletes, whether they're training four times a week or 14 times a week, need to have an endurance focused training session which is done primarily at low heart rates.

These long, slow, endurance building workouts are the perfect opportunity to increase our ability to burn fat, providing we fuel correctly.

You will really be able to ramp up your ability to burn fat as fuel if you keep these endurance building workouts to low heart rates and eliminate carb intake. I am not recommending you do these workouts fasted; that would be a form of under-fueling and could lead to hormonal problems. Instead, keep your calories high and your carbs low.

When training for Challenge Roth, my four to six-hour weekend rides became standard during the final two months before the race. My caloric intake before and during the ride was as follows:

- Breakfast: Coffee with MCT powder, protein powder, and ghee (270 calories/1 gram of carbs)
- Pre-workout snack: 2 tablespoons of natural, no-sugar nut butter (170 calories/8 grams of carbs)

- Fluids during ride: 5 servings of SFuels (225 calories/ 0 grams of carbs)
- Calories during ride: keto bars and natural, no-sugar nut butters (500 calories/20 grams of carbs)

TOTAL: 1,125 calories/29 grams of carbs
(116 calories from carbs)

Contrast this carb intake against what most triathletes would do: eating 60 to 80 grams of carbs before their workout, then having 40 to 60 grams of carbs with their fluid, and 60 grams of carbs every hour during that long ride. This totals upwards of 440 grams of carbs, providing 1,760 calories from carbs, for the entire workout.

Based on the nutrition calculator, this ride requires somewhere in the range of 900 to 1,300 calories. In the case of the traditional carb fueling strategy, you can see the required calories come from carbs, and then some! With that many carbs, there's no reason for your body to even think about touching fat as fuel, so the ability to burn fat isn't developed. In fact, it's reduced. But in the case of fueling with fewer carbs, you still get the calories you require, but just a small fraction of those calories come from carbs and the balance will be forced to come from fat. Your body will learn how to burn fat as fuel, and you'll be much stronger for it come race day.

There are a couple things to note with this approach in order to make it work.

First, these long rides and runs need to be done at a low intensity, probably lower than you're currently training. This means training in your aerobic heart training zone; on Team Trainiac, we have a physiological test and a calculator to work out each athlete's individual exact aerobic training zone, but you can approximate yours with the following calculation:

220 - your age x 0.75 = top end of aerobic training zone

Keeping your heart rate under this ceiling will be challenging at first, particularly on the run. But after several months of consistent workouts, your pace at that low heart rate will drop and faster efforts will feel easier. This is a topic for an entirely separate book, but trust me, being successful in 70.3 and IRONMAN racing isn't about being able to have a fast top-end speed, it's about making your easy efforts faster.

The second thing to keep in mind when you start doing lower carb endurance efforts is you should ease into it. Don't eliminate carbs then go out for a five-hour ride. Start by holding off carbs until two hours into a ride, then 2.5 hours, then 3, and so on. Eventually you'll get to a point where you can even leave the house for a five-hour ride with nothing in your pocket besides a phone and a flat repair kit, your body becomes so good at burning fat that the calories almost become an afterthought.

CARBS PRIOR TO INTENSE WORKOUTS

This is where periodizing your carbs comes into play. Just like not all workouts should be easy efforts, not all workouts should be fuelled with lower carbs. Those two or three less intense workouts done at a low heart rate that you do each week are perfect for fat burning, but your harder speed and strength building workouts are intended to really challenge your body's top end abilities. You'll need easy to access fuel (carbs) to do that.

Prior to your key harder workouts, you'll want to provide your body with 30 to 40 grams of long-lasting complex carbohydrates. You're looking at giving your body just enough carbs to perform at a high level during a hard workout; 30 to 40 grams is a good amount.

Rather than filling your body with simple sugars and carbohydrates which might cause a sudden spike in blood sugar followed by a rapid crash, consume complex carbohydrates which digest much more slowly. Complex carbs still provide a good amount of energy, it's just released more gradually so the energy lasts longer, and the energy crash isn't as drastic.

Below is a graph produced by UCAN SuperStarch (a product I use and recommend. This recommendation is my own, I am not paid to promote this product). UCAN SuperStarch is an incredibly complex carbohydrate; complex carbohydrates are carbs that take a long time to break down so the energy spike they cause is lower and the crash afterwards is lower. As you can see, SuperStarch is so complex the blood sugar graph is nearly flat. Choose complex carbs that provide this type of long-lasting energy.

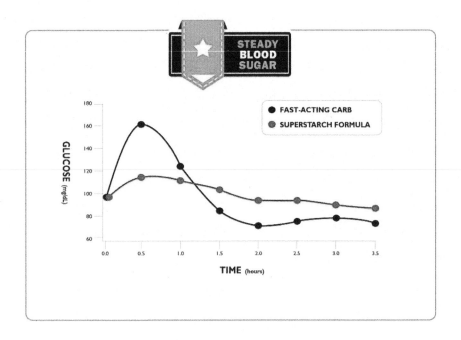

Typical sources of pre-workout complex carbs:

✓ Oats

✓ Quinoa cereal (don't add a sugary milk)

✓ Potatoes and sweet potatoes (potato pancakes)

✓ UCAN SuperStarch products

✓ Brown and wild rice

When I want carbs, my most common breakfasts are decaf coffee with protein powder, MCT powder, and ghee with a UCAN SuperStarch carb on the side. Or, if I'm preparing for a longer workout of 3 or more hours, I'll have 1/3 cup gluten-free steel cut oats with a scoop of UCAN SuperStarch mixed in.

INCORPORATE CARBS IN THE WEEKS LEADING UP TO A RACE

If you're following this low carb training approach, you'll find you won't be taking in a huge amount of carbs during most workouts. But we want to follow the "train low, race high" approach where our training is done with lower carbs, and our racing is done with higher carbs.

We don't want to show up on race day without having consumed a higher amount of carbs. So, in the six weeks leading up to a race, we want to incorporate typical sports nutrition carbohydrates into one workout per week.

At six weeks out from a race, select the workout you do each week that most resembles your race effort. This is usually the weekend long ride followed by a brick run OR it could be a mid-week, race pace interval ride followed by a brick run; you'll know which workout is most "race like."

During this workout, practice taking in calories and fluids on the exact schedule with the same products we planned out in the "Calculate Your Nutrition" section of this book. Practicing your nutrition in the weeks leading up to the race, but maintaining a lower daily carbohydrate intake and still having a few lower intensity workouts a week done with fewer carbs, will train your gut and stomach to take on the fuel you'll need during the race while still being able to burn a high amount of fat.

This strategy will result in a strong performance right up to the finish line with minimal chance of bonking or stomach problems.

BONUS: THREE WEEK COLD KETO

If you're into this idea of using a lower carb approach to triathlon training, and you want to increase your body's ability to use fat as fuel in a hurry, instead of doing it gradually, you can incorporate a three week, "cold keto" forced adaptation phase.

Athletes, including me, can certainly become better at burning fat as fuel without ever having to go through a strict carb restriction period. But some people prefer to make a drastic shift and see results as quickly as possible. This quick protocol also has the benefit of showing athletes a distinct before and after so they can assess how they felt and performed before and after carb restriction; changes in a more gradual approach might occur so slowly that the athlete won't even notice the changes.

Being able to see a distinct before and after is helpful because not everyone will do well on a lower carb diet. Women over 40, for example, tend not to do as well with a carb restricted approach as larger men under 30.

Performing this strict three-week keto adaptation phase essentially forces your body to learn to burn fat as fuel. The method we recommend is the protocol I went through while working with Dr. Dan Plews. It is well researched and has been implemented successfully with many athletes.

Here is how to do it:

- Start with a three-week cleansing diet eating nothing but Whole 30 foods.

  ✓ During this time, don't worry about restricting carbs or protein, or increasing fat. Eat what you feel like eating as long as it's on the Whole 30 foods list. This list is easily found by Googling "Whole 30."

  ✓ Track your food intake through an app like Senza so you start to understand what your diet will need to be once you're fully taking a lower carb approach.

- After the three-week cleanse, proceed into a three-week cold keto phase, restricting carbs to less than 50 grams per day.

  ✓ Consume only foods that are Whole 30.

✓ Keep protein levels at 1.9 to 2 grams of protein per kilogram of bodyweight. I know this is against what a lot of keto people recommend but:

    a) we're not aiming for a traditional keto approach; carb restriction is the key thing; and

    b) endurance athletes require a high amount of protein to maintain muscle fibers.

- Workouts during the cold keto phase:

✓ Keep training levels normal during this period but drop almost all intensity down to Zone 1 or 2 in your aerobic range.

✓ Do one HIIT training session on the bike each week. This session will feel awful, but it's important to stimulating hormones to maintain your top end speed and not lose it, which happens to a lot of people when they go on a lower carb diet.

During both these phases, eat when you're hungry and don't worry about calorie restriction or addition. But if you've historically had a hard time with overeating or underrating, a good rule of thumb for daily required calories can be found at http://mitokinetics.com/mitocalc.html, which is one of the most accurate caloric burn calculators I know of.

After this three-week period, bring your carbs back up to an average of 100 to 150 grams of carbs per day. You can certainly continue eating a Whole 30 diet, but it's not as critical at this point. Just focus on fewer processed foods whenever possible.

If you've followed all these simple changes 75 to 85% of the time or more, but not stressed about being militant with your diet, you will certainly make huge improvements in your triathlon performances. You will likely:

✓ Have steady energy to the finish line of any distance race.

✓ Recover more quickly.

✓ Have less likelihood of bonking or having stomach discomfort in a race.

✓ Find your muscles will be more durable and encounter less breakdown during long races or workouts.

✓ Pass dozens if not hundreds of your competitors towards the end of a race.

✓ Find your races won't hinge on hitting every single last perfect bit of your nutrition plan exactly right because you'll be more metabolically resilient.

✓ Most importantly, you'll be healthier overall because you won't be consuming hundreds of pounds of simple sugars every single year.

The system we've laid out is a great plan, but as Mike Tyson says, "everyone has a plan until they get punched in the mouth." I recognize the plan we've worked out might seem easy on paper, but when it comes to executing it, there will be challenges on race day or during training that will cause you to ask questions.

What do you do if you calculate your calorie intake intervals and the math works out where you need to take a hit of calories both 12 minutes from the end of the bike AND 10 minutes from the end of the bike? What if you get into the race and despite doing everything according to plan, you just don't want to eat? How are you supposed to carry this giant buffet while you're racing?

In the next section, we'll touch on some of the ways you can massage your custom nutrition plan to make it executable on race day, no matter what nuances the race delivers to you. You'll know what proper race nutrition is and how to dodge the punches that may get thrown your way on race day.

CARRYING YOUR NUTRITION

If you've read *Triathlon Bike Foundations*, you know how important keeping a nice, clean, aerodynamic bike is, but how are you supposed to keep your bike aerodynamic if you've got to carry enough food to choke a yak?

Let's start by dealing with your fluids. As we mentioned earlier, the best places to carry your fluids are in a horizontal bottle between your aerobars, a 45-degree cage behind your seat, or with a downtube-mounted bottle specially designed for your bike.

I'm personally not a fan of big water bottles that hang down below your aerobars because they catch the wind, throwing your front wheel around, thus creating a less stable bike. This causes you to lose power and build fatigue in the upper body as you work to keep the bike straight.

Good options:

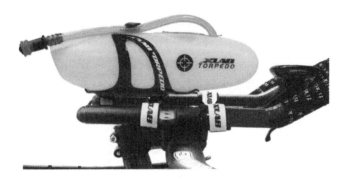

Less desirable options:

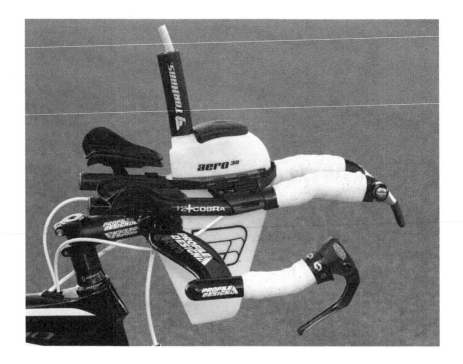

When it comes to carrying your calories, there are really only two places to put them: in your tri suit back pockets or in a bento box mounted to your bike.

Items placed in your tri suit pockets and aren't dangling out loosely are essentially impervious to the wind. Bento boxes secured to the top tube of your bike either toward the seat post or toward the stem are in a "noisy air" area because the pumping of your knees is disturbing the wind in that spot anyway. In other words, putting a bento box there doesn't ruin an aerodynamically optimized area.

You can put all your nutrition in your tri suit and underneath your wetsuit, so there's nothing to do in transition. You can even pre-open all the items you'll put into your bento box, saving time in transition. During Challenge Roth, I emptied all my Clif Blocks into my bento box without any packaging so they were ready to eat immediately.

Bento Box

Running with nutrition might seem a little more complicated but it doesn't need to be.

As we mentioned earlier, liquids are the preferable source of both calories and fluids when running. Consuming gels, chews, or bars during the run is not recommended because they're going to sit in your stomach and be harder to digest, potentially causing GI distress.

One thing I don't recommend is running with a bottle in your hand, even if it is strapped in. Running with one bottle creates an imbalance in the sides of your body and can create an asymmetric running stride and injuries. Running with a bottle in each hand solves this asymmetry issue but when your legs get tired during the run, you'll have to rely on your pumping arms to keep your pace going. If you've got bottles weighing your arms down, you won't have a way to push through the fatigue.

If you have a specific liquid you want to bring along to the run, I recommend preparing it in a small, super-concentrated flask that you can put in your tri suit back pockets or on a running belt that you put on while jogging gently out of Transition 2. You can take this super concentrate of calories on your calculated intervals and wash it down with a little water from aid stations to help digest it easily.

Personally, I like using good old Coca-Cola for my calories while on the run because just about every single race provides it. You know what it's going to taste like, it's very easy to digest, it has some sodium to replace your lost electrolytes, and it features caffeine to give you a little extra kick as you start to get tired. If you choose to use this method, once you start drinking Coke, don't stop or you'll crash hard. I used nothing but Coke and water throughout the entire 42.2 kilometers of my run in Challenge Roth.

Finally, for your fluids, I recommend a mixture of on-course water and on-course electrolytes. You can find out what will be on course ahead of the race and, if it's a light electrolyte drink that you know you'll digest well, you can confidently drink that at every aid station.

If the on-course electrolyte drink is something you're not familiar with, try a sip of the electrolyte drink at the first aid station and see if it's super sweet. If it is really sweet, it's probably too concentrated and has a high number of calories. In this case, grab the electrolyte plus some water at every aid station to dilute the electrolyte in your stomach and make it easier to digest.

During training, it helps to occasionally try different sports nutrition products to develop a little bit of durability in your gut, so you can successfully consume whatever nutrition products are provided on course.

BURPING OR AN UPSET STOMACH

Let's say you've done all the training, you've done all your calculations and scheduling of the nutrition, you've got the nutrition schedule burned into your memory and the sports products are packed to be as aero as possible. But then you get into the race and things aren't sitting right in your stomach, you're burping constantly, and your stomach is doing backflips.

Don't worry, this happens to a lot of athletes. During intense exercise, your digestive system nearly shuts down, and sure, maybe you've consumed fluids and calories in the training leading up to the race, but you likely haven't gone as hard for as long a stretch. It's tremendously hard for your stomach to function at a high level, and it's not uncommon for burping or an upset stomach to occur.

If this ends up happening, I want you to keep taking calories on your planned schedule, but I want you to switch from your electrolyte drink to straight water to change the osmolality in your stomach (I mentioned this earlier, this very thing happened to me during Challenge Roth in 2019). Hopefully this helps alleviate the problems you're having, but if the problem persists, take slightly less fluid until the issue gets better.

Finally, if you've switched to water and decreased the amount of fluid you're taking in, but you're still having stomach issues, there's a chance it just might not be your day, and you're just going to have to grind it out to the finish. We're putting our bodies through a pretty brutal thing when we do triathlons, and it's not always going to go well. However, with the system we've laid out, the likelihood of this happening is much lower.

If this happens to you regularly, you might be an excellent candidate for a low carb approach to training. The stomach issues might be occurring because your stomach can't process enough material to fuel your efforts, and increasing the amount of fat you burn will allow you to take in fewer calories, which will take the load off your stomach.

DON'T FEEL LIKE EATING

In addition to burping and an upset stomach, another common issue is not feeling like eating. Athletes often lose their appetite in a race, particularly in hot weather, because more blood leaves the stomach and goes to the surface of the skin to cool us down.

If you're in a race and don't feel like eating, it's a bit more challenging than burping and an upset stomach, because it may mean your stomach doesn't even want to consider working.

If you're in a spot where you don't feel like eating, this doesn't mean you don't need to eat. It's not like in day-to-day eating where eating only when you're hungry is a good idea. During a race, you need fuel. You're burning a HUGE number of calories and you need to replace calories, there's no way around it. The best way to fix the issue of not wanting to eat is by preventing it from happening in the first place.

You can reduce the likelihood of this by making sure that in the six weeks leading up to race day, you train at least one day per week with your planned race nutrition. This will train your gut to function while exercising.

You can also reduce the likelihood of losing your appetite by sticking to a proper race nutrition plan... like the one laid out in this book.

Finally, you need to be very in tune with your body during the race. You need to pay as much attention to your nutrition plan and how your body and stomach are feeling as you pay to your power or pace. If you can recognize stomach discomfort or burping early on, you'll be able to switch to straight water to help settle your gut down before it ruins your race.

If, despite all that you still can't regain your appetite, try to force feed yourself small amounts of the tastiest food you've packed, or whatever you can get at aid stations on the course. Switch to water and a salt tab or salt stick for fluids. If all that fails, as I said above, you might be having a hard day and you'll just have to grind out to the finish.

CRANKY

"Oh geez, this race is so long, and I'm feeling so bad. This is never going to go well."

"My power is dropping, I screwed up my training. Coach Taren sucks!"

"Why did I enter this race? This is stupid. I'm never going to do another triathlon again."

Sound familiar? Lots of triathletes experience negative self-talk during the race, saying nastier things to ourselves than we'd say to our worst enemy. A little bit of negative chatter is okay, but sustained, depressing, negative self-talk is not.

Fortunately, this can be an easy fix. Take more carbs. Lots of them, right away!

Quite often this negative self-talk is the brain's first line of defence when it's deprived of glucose. Just like how the brain might initiate cramping in the body if the physical effort is approaching a dangerous level (well, what the brain might think is dangerous but really isn't), it has a similar mental self-defence mechanism if we're not functioning well mentally.

The brain needs sugars to function properly during intense exercise, so if you start feeling down about the race, get some easy-to-access carbs in your system like Coke or a gel with caffeine. It should help to perk you up.

IRREGULAR INTERVALS

Let's say you've gone through all the calculations and you've figured out you need to take calories every 22 minutes, which should result in perfect feeding intervals on the bike. You get to the race and feel great, your training went well and you're perfectly tapered, feeling like a caged animal just waiting to show the world how hard you've worked. You get out of the swim and head out on the bike, nailing your nutrition. But you quickly realize there's a problem. You're performing so well that you're biking faster than you expected when you did your nutrition plan calculations. This unexpected speed-up is going to result in one of the 22-minute feeding intervals landing just four minutes before the planned feeding interval that happens 10 minutes from the end of the bike.

If this happens, don't worry. While the system we've outlined is based on exact science, racing is not an exact science. Personally, I've never had a race where the actual nutrition I consumed was the same as what I had planned. I've always had some stomach gurgles or left a few extra Clif Blocks in my bento box, because the intervals didn't work out perfectly. I've even had to take Red Bull in the final 7 kilometers of one run to snap some energy back into my legs (FYI, this is a last resort and only for the very end of the race).

If you get into the race and your nutrition plan ends up resulting in irregular intervals, this is where your body awareness needs to kick in so you can make decisions on the fly. If you feel a little tired or cranky, adjust your intervals so you get in just few more calories. If you feel great, you're killing it, you feel strong and have consumed every last bit of your planned nutrition, adjust the feeding intervals to take in slightly fewer calories.

If you're making these on-the-fly decisions in a race, there are a few intervals to make sure you stick to:

Sprint, Olympic, 70.3: 20 minutes before the race, 10 minutes into the bike, 10 minutes before Transition 2, and 10 minutes after Transition 2.

IRONMAN: 20 minutes before the race, Transition 1, 10 minutes before Transition 2, 10 minutes after Transition 2.

Make sure to maintain these feeding intervals and adjust the other feeding times around them.

CAFFEINE

A lot of triathletes believe they shouldn't drink coffee or take in any caffeine on race day because they don't want to get dehydrated. Others get as jacked up on caffeine as they possibly can in hopes that they'll turn into the Incredible Hulk.

Caffeine is one of the few substances which, in the right circumstances, is an accepted performance enhancer. Various studies have shown that caffeine increases top end speed, enhances endurance, increases the ability to burn fat, and decreases perception of pain. It's one of the only legal performance enhancers that provides a true benefit. Here's how to use caffeine most effectively.

If you're someone who drinks coffee every day, have your cup of coffee the morning of the race. Not having your cup of coffee may result in a worse performance because your body is being deprived of something it's accustomed to having. Don't worry about dehydration -- it's been shown that coffee is pretty much neutral on hydration meaning that you will be out some fluids, but those fluids are offset by the coffee you consumed.

If you do regularly drink coffee, and you continued to drink coffee each day leading up to the race, you won't see much performance enhancing benefit from taking huge amounts of caffeine during the race. If you want to use caffeine as a performance enhancer (which it is, and a damn good one), you'll need to go on a caffeine cleanse for three weeks before the race. Then, when you get into the race the return of caffeine in your system will feel like rocket fuel!

If you're someone who doesn't ingest caffeine normally, you can certainly use caffeinated sports nutrition products when you race. Since you don't typically have caffeine, you'll probably see a boost in performance. However, if you don't regularly have caffeine, you'll want to test it during training to make sure you don't experience any significant negative side effects.

HOT WEATHER

Hot weather is a triathlete's kryptonite. Even a talented professional triathlete like 2019 Kona podium finisher Sarah Crowley, who grew up in Australia, which she claims is hotter and harder to train in than Kona, goes to the IRONMAN World Championship in Hawaii and puts out significantly slower times than she does in other races.

Our performance declines in hot weather because our heart rate increases at the same effort levels, while pumping more blood to the surface of the skin to cool us. Because more blood is at the surface of the skin, there's less blood in our stomachs with which to digest calories and fluids. So, triathletes often think, "It's hot, I'm sweating a lot, I have to guzzle more fluids." They're not entirely wrong, but they might be setting themselves up for digestive problems if they don't guzzle properly.

You won't be able to go from 26 ounces of fluids every hour to 32 ounces of fluids every hour the very next day. So, in the weeks leading up to a hot race, you'll have to increase your fluid intake during workouts, training your gut to accept that larger amount of liquid.

Next, when game time comes around and you're racing in hot weather, you'll want to drink as much as possible while keeping the principles we've discussed top of mind. Drink as much as possible, but if your stomach starts feeling funny, switch to water. If you're noticing burping or sloshing, decrease the amount of fluid you take in. Drink as much as you can while not causing discomfort.

This isn't related to nutrition, but if you're going to be racing in a hot weather race, you can alleviate some of the hurt that will occur by using a sauna as part of your training, and changing when you do some of your workouts. Starting six to eight weeks out from the race, and stopping when your taper starts, try to perform your easy workouts during the hottest part of the day wherever you live. Or, if you train inside, try leaving all the windows closed and don't use any fans.

A more powerful method of heat preparation which is backed by science and used by pro triathletes Trevor and Heather Wurtele, both who perform very well in heat, is to go into the sauna three times a week immediately after your last hard workout of the day. Start with 10 minutes in the sauna and build up to 30 minutes. But here's the hard part and the key: DO NOT hydrate before or during your sauna session. Let yourself suffer through that tiny bit of dehydration, then hydrate aggressively after your sauna.

These two tactics will increase your blood plasma levels so more oxygen will be transported to the muscles, and you'll develop the ability to start sweating more quickly, making it easier to cool your body on race day.

CRAMPING

We discussed cramping earlier and talked about how cramping is less about nutrition and more about the effort level you're putting out, as perceived by the brain. Even if you pace your race perfectly and nail your nutrition, you might still encounter cramping. This is completely normal and nothing you should feel bad about. Even three-time IRONMAN World Champion Craig Alexander had severe cramps at the end of his run when he set the course record at the 2011 IRONMAN World Championship in Kona, Hawaii.

Cramps will almost certainly come at some point if you race enough triathlons, so here are some strategies to deal with them.

As I mentioned previously, cramps are believed to arise from a signal in the brain and not something that's necessarily functionally wrong in the body. So, we need a way to reset the brain and snap it out of its hissy fit. Boxers use smelling salts to wake themselves up during a fight and weightlifters use smelling salts to get themselves hyper-aware before a big lift. Before you go out and buy a bunch of smelling salts to keep in your jersey pocket, don't bother; I've researched this, and it doesn't enhance endurance performance. Shucks, hey?

Again, as we touched upon, a triathlete's version of smelling salts that's been shown to work is strong-tasting food. Some use a salt stick. It's straight salt from a tube; athletes lick their thumb, shake some salt onto that wet thumb, then lick their thumb go get the potent taste of salt. An option I've used, which is an even bigger punch in the mouth, is a vinegar supplement like Pickle Juice or CrampFix. These are so strong tasting that I coughed up half a CrampFix packet about 14 kilometers into the Challenge Roth run course. But the cramps went away instantly, and I was back in the fight.

The key to fighting off cramps with products like Base Salt or CrampFix is to start taking them before the cramp settles in. This is again where you need to be in tune with your body during the race. I find that towards the end of the bike, little "peanuts" of tension start to show up in my legs. This is the start of cramps for me, so when these peanuts show up, it's a good time to take a brain reset product to hopefully prevent the cramp from taking hold. On the run, cramps can come on strong and often, so I like to carry a Base Salt tube with me in my tri suit or in my hand to constantly keep those cramps in check. This method has the added benefit of getting some electrolytes in so you can take water on the run course and not have to risk using whatever random electrolyte drink is offered on the course.

OTHER RANDOM ISSUES

You now have all the tools you need to make sure nutrition is never holding you back from your best possible race. But, of course, there will be some of you who have unique circumstances that don't easily fit within the guidelines we've laid out, or those who try these methods and find you're still having issues.

In this section, we'll touch briefly on some of the unique circumstances triathletes encounter due to genetics or lifestyle choices. In a lot of cases, you may have to continue to experiment in order to find what works for you. If that's the case, don't completely abandon all the guidelines we've outlined! Keep the guidelines in mind and see if you can use them to find an answer that's right for you.

If there are unique requirements you're dealing with that I haven't dealt with, please message me online with an explanation of what you're working through. I likely won't have an immediate answer for you, but if I see that enough people are dealing with a certain challenge, I'll be able to update this section in future versions of this book to help you and other athletes.

BEET JUICE

Beet juice has been the rage for endurance athletes for the past several years. The thought is that the nitrates in beets open the blood vessels, allowing more blood to flow and thus helping us a achieve a better performance.

I've discussed this with one PhD candidate and one PhD who both researched the effectiveness of beet juice and both said beets have a positive effect on performance, but only for approximately 30% of the population.

If you try beet juice and notice a significant improvement in your performance, congratulations, you just won the genetic beet juice lottery! Feel free to include beets/beet juice/beetroot powder in your nutrition plan. But if you don't notice much benefit, or you notice just a marginal benefit, you're likely not in that lucky one-third of the population, and any performance benefit you're experiencing is probably a short-lived placebo. In that case, save your money.

GLUCOSE, FRUCTOSE, SUCROSE, OR MALTODEXTRIN

I mentioned earlier that maltodextrin is the preferred source of carbohydrates in a race. This is because maltodextrin is very easy to digest. That said, it requires more fluid to digest so it sucks some of the fluid out of the blood and body, and into the gut, potentially leading to hydration issues.

Some athletes might point out that if you combine glucose and fructose you can increase the amount of carbs you consume each hour from 60 grams to 90 grams. This is correct, but fructose is very hard for the human stomach to digest and is more likely to lead to gut problems in the race. Furthermore, we've already discussed how our stomachs are challenged just to consume 60 grams of carbs per hour, do you really think increasing that number by 50% is a risk you want to take?

I used Hammer Nutrition Perpetuem in both open water marathon swims I completed because its primary carb source was maltodextrin. In both cases, I was able to get in enough calories, without any gut issues, but in the following days I felt incredibly dry. During the bike portion of Challenge Roth in 2019, I fueled primarily with Clif Blocks, and again I felt very dry for a few days after the race.

It's important to note, as indicated by Dr. Stacy Sims, Stanford PhD, and founder of Osmo Nutrition, women can't absorb maltodextrin as easily as men.

While I recommend looking into maltodextrin-based carbohydrate sources, before you ever use it in a race, try it in training to see how you feel. If you can use a maltodextrin-based sports nutrition product without any noticeable negative effects in training, it will likely be okay during racing.

HUNGER DURING LONG WORKOUTS OR EVENTS

Some athletes have told me they get hungry during their training. If this sounds like you, you're not alone.

As I noted earlier, pro triathlete and two-time Olympian Sarah True told me when she stepped up to long distance racing, she didn't know how to fuel because she had spent a lifetime doing ITU short-course racing where race nutrition was an afterthought. She said she often just forgot to eat in a 70.3, and would feel incredibly hungry during the run, and her performance would deteriorate. This performance decline occurred despite trying to eat once she felt hungry, but by then it was too late.

If you find you're getting hungry, it likely means you've under-fuelled coming into the race, or you are under-fuelling during the race. The simple solution for this is: don't go into a hard effort fasted or under-fuelled, and stick to the calculations and schedules we've helped you create.

POOR FAT METABOLIZER

While I've painted a low carb approach to training as a potential solution to all of your nutritional problems, people are on a spectrum and the low carb/high fat approach may not be for you.

Some athletes are like Jan Van Berkel or Dr. Dan Plews and function extremely well with as few as at 100 grams of carbs per day, while some athletes may not perform well at this level at all.

You can see on the Performance Fitness Concepts website, headed by Dr. Phil Goglia, an expert in performance nutrition, that 74% of people metabolize fat and protein the best, 23% metabolize carbohydrates the best, and only 3% metabolize both equally well.

So, there's certainly a chance you may not perform well with a lower carb approach. It takes roughly 10 to 12 weeks to get a performance adaptation to the low carb approach, and years to get the full benefits. If after two weeks of lower carbs you don't feel great, don't be surprised. But if after four months your performance numbers still aren't improving, you don't feel like easy aerobic efforts can go on all day, and you're seeing no performance improvements, low carb might not be for you.

As explained to me by Dr. Dan Plews when we began our low carb project together, "Low carb could be to the solution to all your problems, or the cause of a whole bunch more."

MEDICALLY ADVISED LOW CARB

Some athletes are on medically advised (and monitored) low carbohydrate diets, full-on, lifelong keto diet carbs restricted to as low as 20 grams or less per day.

2012 IRONMAN World Champion Pete Jacobs struggled with bouts of fatigue and overtraining issues since he was 15 years old. We talked to Pete on the Triathlon Taren Podcast in 2019 after he was able to identify that both he and his mother were experiencing severe auto-immune reactions to lectins in plants that caused inflammation, gut distress, and fatigue. Pete told us that he and his mom ended up going full carnivore, where the only thing that pass across their lips are eggs, meat, fish, water, and salt. Pete said he felt better than he can ever remember feeling in his life and he was performing better than he had in years.

Does that mean you should eliminate all carbs or plants and go on a carnivore diet? Probably not. But this example shows there is a tiny fraction of the population who may have a genetic or medically identified reason to eliminate carbs altogether. If this happens to be you, you might still be able to do triathlon.

But and this is a big but, if you are restricting carbohydrates for any reason to below 50 grams of carbs per day on an ongoing basis, I'd certainly recommend enlisting in the help of some professionals to monitor your situation. Low carb proponent Dr.

Grant Schofield explained on our podcast that being in ketosis for months on end, particularly for an endurance athlete, is risky.

If severe carb restriction is something you are forced to do, make sure you're doing frequent hormone tests to ensure you're staying healthy. Even if you feel fine, your hormones could be suffering and it's typically not until it's too late you know your hormones have taken a beating. Once hormones get thrown off, it takes a lot of time and effort to bring them back into balance.

SIDE NOTE: I over-trained and developed hormonal problems in 2017 that, as of writing this in 2020, I'm still working to fix.

ALLERGIES, VEGAN, VEGETARIAN, PALEO, ETC.

Finally, I must acknowledge there are a huge number of dietary lifestyles, allergies, and philosophies that are common around the world.

Personally, I eat gluten-free and I even dabbled in eating mostly vegan meals for a couple of years. *To clarify a common misconception that often comes up in the comments on my social media channels: I was never fully vegan, but 85-90% of my food intake was plant-based.* I respect a lot of people have different dietary choices and I don't judge any of those decisions.

Addressing how to fuel in a race, in training, and day-to-day for every gluten-free, dairy-free, sugar-free, vegan, food sensitive, Halal-eating athlete out there would require a book about 10 times the size of this one. That's why I've tried to write this book with broad-based principles that, regardless of what your dietary choices are, you can use to customize your own diet.

Use the tips and tools in this book as guidelines, not rules that are never meant to be broken, but to find a plan that works for you.

CHAPTER 7

MOVING FORWARD

As I was on the run course of Challenge Roth, my first full IRONMAN distance race, I was astounded by how many people I passed as they pulled up to walk, even during the first 10 kilometers of the run. These athletes had ignored nutrition so badly on the bike that their race was done before the run even started.

Further into the run, as the halfway mark approached, those walkers turned into people who were limping with cramps, or throwing up on the side of the road. Even deeper into the run, during the final 15 kilometers, the carnage continued with athletes coming in and out of the bushes, dealing with their respective gut disasters. Meanwhile, I was clipping off five-minute kilometers like clockwork, without stopping or having any serious gut problems, for all 42.2 kilometers.

I'd heard the tales of how many athletes experienced these problems in IRONMAN races but I had no idea how common it was. What's more, if all these athletes were experiencing such problems in IRONMAN, where small issues become huge problems, think about how much the athletes were underperforming in their shorter races where an improper nutrition plan doesn't result in such disasters but certainly results in worse performance.

The unfortunate fact of triathlon is that we all spend a bulk of our spare time swimming, biking, running, and doing strength or injury prevention work. Then we have jobs to go to (in order to pay for all of our sexy tri gear) and real lives to keep afloat. With only so many hours in a day to dedicate to this sport, race nutrition often ends up being an afterthought.

The goal of this book is to help you figure out race nutrition without having to take a ton of time to do it. As I've said a few times, there is a very handy calculator provided at https://triathlontaren.com/nutritionfoundations/ which will do most of the work for you. The reality is, we all must fuel ourselves in training and during a race, and there's no point putting in all of that dedicated training if we're going to throw it away with improper nutrition. Don't let your fuel be an afterthought. Fuel yourself with a system that will support good performance!

Now, Trainiac, you *almost* have all the knowledge you'll need to move forward and make nutrition a weapon in your races. If you follow the system laid out in this book, you'll have tools to deal with cramping, you'll have steady energy, you'll feel strong crossing the finish line, you shouldn't experience gut distress during races, your training will be well-absorbed making you fitter, stronger, and faster, and you'll step up to the start line of every race feeling confident.

I say you've got *"almost"* all of the knowledge because this system, while it's based on science and the successful implementation by thousands of Trainiacs around the world, is not 100% foolproof. You need to test and customize this system to make sure it works for your body's unique needs.

With that in mind here's how you can move forward with the tools laid out in this book:

Step 1: Perform the calculations and scheduling you've just learned about.

Step 2: Try the nutrition plan derived from Step 1 in your longer bike/run brick workouts.

Step 3: As you're trying the nutrition plan, experiment with different kinds of nutritional products to see what tastes good and sits well in your stomach. You can use multiple products within the same workout or try different sports nutrition products across multiple workouts.

Step 4: Learn your body and how much fluids and calories are exactly right for you. Drink as much as possible until you notice burping or sloshing in your stomach, then scale back. Eat based on your calculated nutrition from this system. If you feel sluggish towards the end of hard workouts, you might need a little more. If you feel like food is sitting in your stomach, you might need a little less.

Step 5: Pay attention to all the cues your body is giving you during training and use the strategies from this book to recognize issues on race day and address them before they become bigger problems.

Take all the knowledge, tools, calculators, schedules, and guidelines laid out in this book and go turn race nutrition into a weapon that's as equally strong as your strongest discipline. If you choose to use the system and guidelines laid out here, I guarantee you'll be able to make sure nutrition is never the factor holding you back from a successful race.

Later, Trainiac!

MY FUELING SCHEDULE FROM A FEW RECENT RACES

CHALLENGE DAYTONA SPRINT: 1:05

- 20 minutes prior to race: 1 gel with caffeine
- 10 minutes into bike until 10 minutes from end of bike: sipped light electrolyte drink
- 5 minutes after Transition 2 until end of run: sipped electrolyte drink at each aid station

NOTE: If your race is longer than 80 minutes, you will likely have to take some calories but for a 65-minute event, I basically just make sure I don't feel thirsty by sipping a light electrolyte drink.

BIRDS HILL OLYMPIC 2018: 2:11:25

- 20 minutes prior to race: 1 gel with caffeine

- 10 minutes into bike until 10 minutes from end of bike: two Clif Blocks every 20 minutes

- 1 bottle of SOS electrolytes on bike

- 5 minutes after Transition 2 until end of run: sipped electrolyte drink at each aid station

- 25 minutes into run: took a gel, watered down with a big sip of water from an aid station

ATLANTIC CITY 70.3 2019: 4:28

- 20 minutes prior to race: 1 UCAN energy bar with caffeine

- 10 minutes into bike until 10 minutes from end of bike: two Clif Blocks every 20 minutes

- 1.6 liters of SOS electrolytes on bike and another half-liter of water taken over the course of two water bottle grabs at aid stations, placed roughly at 30 kilometers into the bike and 60 kilometers into the bike

- Halfway through bike, swapped a serving of two Clif Blocks for one Verb Energy bar to get some solid foods in and not feel hungry

- 10 minutes from end of bike: 1 serving of CrampFix to wake myself up

- 5 minutes after Transition 2 until end of run: Took a solid drink of Coke at every aid station, switching to water any time my stomach felt like it was sloshing around

CHALLENGE ROTH FULL IRONMAN DISTANCE 2019: 9:41:35

- 20 minutes prior to race: 1 Verb energy bar with caffeine

- Transition 1: 90 calories of Coke

- Every 20 minutes thereafter on the bike:
  - ✓ 2 Clif Blocks or 1/2 of a Picky bar with caffeine (I consumed a total of two Picky Bars during the entire bike)
  - ✓ 2 liters of SOS electrolyte

- A couple instances, I encountered a bit of digestive discomfort, so I grabbed water bottles at the aid stations and drank water until my stomach felt better. I probably consumed likely 2 bottles of straight water.

- 10 minutes from the end of the bike: one serving of CrampFix.

- Starting from 10 minutes into the run and until the very end of the run: Consumed Coke at every single aid station unless my stomach felt funny, in which case I would have water.

- 1 serving of CrampFix at 14 kilometers into the run and again at 28 kilometers into the run.

ACKNOWLEDGEMENTS

Without the help of some very generous people, the system you've just read about would not have been possible to sort out or even get down on paper. I need to acknowledge those who have helped make this happen.

First, even though he doesn't know me or know he's getting thanked, I owe a huge thank you to John Ivy and his book *The Performance Zone*. This is the book that originally helped me through my early nutritional issues and formed the foundation for the nutrition calculator we developed.

Next, thank you to Dr. Dan Plews who trained me to the 9:41 I produced at Challenge Roth in 2019. Dan is one of the best triathlon coaches in the world. Throughout that build to Roth, he taught me how to effectively use low carb training in a safe manner that generates performance results. Low carb endurance training is much more complex than just lowering your carbs, and without Dan's help, I wouldn't have been able to put out that performance or share that experience with those of you reading this.

Dan has a website called EndureIQ.com where he shares his knowledge about endurance training with the world through video courses. The courses are some of the best investments you can make toward your triathlon performance.

Finally, I owe a huge thanks to the person responsible for keeping me fed 24/7: my wife, No Triathlon Kim. Early on in our relationship I tried to do a nice thing and cook her dinner, and the result was a chicken breast that was still pink on the inside. Fortunately, neither of us got sick, but I was banned from the kitchen for life, so Kim makes nearly every meal I eat.

Kim is also a health nut, so every gluten-free, vegan, paleo, Whole 30, low-carb, and nutritional approach I decide to test becomes something she spends a huge amount of time learning about. She then becomes a master chef in each approach. Without Kim, this book would be about how I eat nothing but peanut butter on white bread.

WHAT'S NEXT

Now that you're done with this book, here are some next steps for you.

1. JOIN THE TRAINIAC COMMUNITY

There are so many ways to join the Trainiac community! Here's how:

- ➤ Visit us online at triathlontaren.com for free resources, valuable training info, and more.

- ➤ Visit teamtrainiac.com to sign up for the most accessible triathlon training platform in the world. For a fraction of the price of a one-on-one coach, get a fully customizable, year-round training plan to get you totally prepared for your races, no matter your level of experience!

2. FOLLOW US ON SOCIAL MEDIA

For tips, tricks, training updates and more, follow us on our most active social media channels:

YOUTUBE: youtube.com/triathlontaren

INSTAGRAM: @triathlontaren

FACEBOOK: facebook.com/triathlontaren

3. SUBSCRIBE TO THE TRIATHLON TAREN PODCAST

The top-rated Triathlon podcast in the world on iTunes, the Triathlon Taren Podcast brings you interviews with the who's-who in triathlon including professional triathletes, inspiring age-groupers and more! Download the podcast wherever you get your favorite podcasts.

4. SHARE THIS BOOK

Please write us a review on Amazon or Goodreads and let your fellow triathletes know about us! Spreading the word helps to reach new readers, to grow the Trainiac community, and it allows us to bring you more great resources.

THANK YOU! And we'll see you soon, Trainiac!

ABOUT THE AUTHOR

"Triathlon Taren" Gesell is a triathlete who has become known for his wildly popular Triathlon Taren YouTube channel, Instagram account, and podcast, where he shares tips, tricks, hacks, the latest scientific findings and time-tested knowledge to help age-groupers get to their start lines confident and their finish lines strong. Based in Winnipeg, Canada, Taren is also the head coach of TeamTrainiac.com, a training platform supporting a growing community of triathletes from all around the world.

Find more books by "TRIATHLON TAREN" GESELL on Amazon.com

Triathlon Swimming Foundations

Triathlon Bike Foundations

Triathlon Running Foundations

Made in the USA
Middletown, DE
29 July 2020